THE TRIUMPH OF FAITH

Stories of hope from the Troubles

MARCUS THOMAS

Dedication

To our three daughters, Elspeth, Jo and Angharad

THE TRIUMPH OF FAITH
Copyright © 2022 by Marcus Thomas

ISBN 978-1-915223-16-6

All rights reserved.

No part of this publication may be reproduced, stored in a retrieval system, or transmitted in any form or by any means, electronic, mechanical, photocopying or otherwise, without prior written consent of the publisher except as provided by under United Kingdom copyright law. Short extracts may be used for review purposes with credits given.

Main translation in use: NIV

Scriptures taken from the Holy Bible, New International Version®, NIV®. Copyright © 1973, 1978, 1984, 2011 by Biblica, Inc.™ Used by permission of Zondervan. All rights reserved worldwide. www.zondervan.com The "NIV" and "New International Version" are trademarks registered in the United States Patent and Trademark Office by Biblica, Inc.™

Other translations in use:

Scripture quotations marked NKJV are taken from the New King James Version®. Copyright © 1982 by Thomas Nelson. Used by permission. All rights reserved.

The Amplified Bible, Copyright © 2015 by The Lockman Foundation, La Habra, CA 90631. All rights reserved.

Scripture quotations are taken from the *Holy Bible*, New Living Translation, copyright © 1996, 2004, 2015 by Tyndale House Foundation. Used by permission of Tyndale House Publishers, Inc., Carol Stream, Illinois 60188. All rights reserved.

New American Standard Bible®, Copyright © 1960, 1971, 1977, 1995, 2020 by The Lockman Foundation. All rights reserved.

The ESV® Bible (The Holy Bible, English Standard Version®). ESV® Text Edition: 2016. Copyright © 2001 by Crossway, a publishing ministry of Good News Publishers. The ESV® text has been reproduced in cooperation with and by permission of Good News Publishers. Unauthorized reproduction of this publication is prohibited. All rights reserved

Scripture quotations marked MSG are taken from *THE MESSAGE*, copyright © 1993, 2002, 2018 by Eugene H. Peterson. Used by permission of NavPress. All rights reserved. Represented by Tyndale House Publishers, Inc.

The Holy Bible, Berean Standard Bible, BSB Copyright ©2016, 2020 by Bible Hub Used by Permission. All Rights Reserved Worldwide.

Emphasis within Scripture quotations is the author's own.

Published by

Maurice Wylie Media
Inspirational Christian Publisher

Publishers' statement: Throughout this book the love for our God is such that whenever we refer to Him, we honour with Capitals. On the other hand, when referring to the devil, we refuse to acknowledge him with any honour to the point of violating grammatical rule and withholding capitalisation.

For more information visit: www.MauriceWylieMedia.com

Contents

	Foreword	11
	Acknowledgements	13
	Introduction	15
Chapter 1:	**The Troubles**	**22**
	Stories from the Troubles…	24
	Belfast during the Troubles…	26
	The Border and South Armagh during the Troubles…	28
	Personal Memories…	36
	Living in Northern Ireland…	37
	Memories from friends…	38
	John's story… (1)	38
	John's story… (2)	39
	Neil's Story…	41
	Robin's story…	44
	Suffering in the World…	46
	Where was God in the Troubles?	48

Chapter 2	**The Christian And Suffering**	**50**
	The Mystery that is Suffering…	51
	Story of a Christian from the Troubles…	54
	The Bible and Suffering…	56
	The Sufferings of Jesus…	59
	A Story: What is Possible?	62
Chapter 3	**The Story Of Rodney Wilson**	**67**
	The Wilson family…	70
	The Grief of a Daughter…	72
	Rodney's story…	74
	The Aftermath and the Funeral…	76
	Rodney's Grief…	78
	Mrs Wilson…	79
	Rodney's Faith…	81
	Rodney's Journey of Forgiveness…	82
Chapter 4	**The Story Of Paul Elliott**	**87**
	Who was Trevor Elliott?	90
	Paul Elliott…	92
Chapter 5	**The Story Of Sara-Louise Martin**	**103**
	The Martin Family…	106
	Who was Inspector Brian Martin?	106
	The Funeral of Inspector Brian Martin…	108
	Sara-Louise…	109
	What was your Life like prior to the Tragic Event?	109

	How did you Suffer?	110
	What Cost did you Experience?	111
	Your Early thoughts?	112
	How did Christians Help?	112
	Where were You in Your Thinking?	113
	What Path has your Life taken since the Tragedy?	114
	Suffering and the Christian Faith…	115
Chapter 6	**The Story Of Maggie Burrows**	**117**
	Who was Herbie Burrows?	118
	Maggie Burrow's Family…	120
	The Day of the Bomb…	121
	The Cost and the Questions…	121
	The Fears…	123
	Faith in the Lord Jesus Christ…	124
Chapter 7	**The Story Of David Clements**	**131**
	Who was Billy Clements?	132
	The Bible Reading for the Day…	134
	Where was David?	140
	What about Mrs Clements?	141
	How did David respond?	142
	A Servant of the Lord Jesus Christ…	143
Chapter 8	**More Stories Of Faith**	**149**
	Derek Kidd…	149
	Joseph Wilson…	150

	Ian and Pauline Bothwell…	154
Chapter 9	**Hope Now And For The Future**	**162**
	The Holiness of God…	166
	The Breaking of Bread…	167
	The Present Ministry of Jesus…	169
	The Eternal Viewpoint…	170
	The Practice of Lament…	172
	Forgiveness…	177
	The People of God…	178
	The Holy Spirit…	179
	God is God…	182
	A Story: "It is Well with my Soul"	184
Chapter 10	A Challenge	188
	Contact	190

"I said to myself, 'God will bring into judgment both the righteous and the wicked, for there will be a time for every activity, a time to judge every deed.'"

Ecclesiastes 3:17 (NIV)

Foreword

In 'The Triumph of Faith' Marcus Thomas gives a voice to many whose voice is rarely, if ever, heard ~ those of the Christian Faith who suffered as a result of "The Troubles". Instead of telling the story of an amorphous group, this book gives the stories of individuals who were victim to some of the worst atrocities seen in our land.

As the son of an RUC officer who served through all the years of the Troubles, I can identify with many of the experiences portrayed in this book. Suffering is not a word you hear when the history of this period in Northern Ireland is told. You are more likely to hear words like 'justice', 'equality', 'fairness', as those with political clout further their narrative. Now a different story is being told, one no less real but equally valid.

All in all, 'The Triumph of Faith' gives us a perspective that would otherwise be overlooked. But what shines through is the buoyancy of faith in response to the personal loss and sorrow suffered by so many. How we need to thank God for His grace to His people during their darkest times. The faith and courage of these people will help carry you until the day when all tears will be wiped away and death and suffering will be no more.

Through this book, the testimony of those at the sharp end is heard, and hope is given in the face of seeming hopelessness.

John White
Church of Ireland Rector of Strabane.

Acknowledgements

I am especially grateful to Rodney Wilson, Paul Elliott, Sara-Louise Martin, Maggie Burrows, David Clements, Ian Bothwell and Chris Kidd for their willingness to include their stories in this book.

The contributions from my friends John, John, Neil and Robin to the chapter "The Troubles", are really appreciated and also the material made available by Pastor Philip Seifert.

Andrew Oliver provided invaluable research and background information for the stories included in this book. Thank you, Andrew. You were thorough and efficient in your research.

Thanks also to a number of other people who, in the initial stages, listened to me on the phone, sought to help me uncover stories for this book and perused my first attempts at writing it.

I am grateful to Rector Rev. John White for agreeing to write the foreword to this book. I value his friendship and support.

Thank you to Pat, my wife. Her exactness and skills in the English language have made the book readable.

I would like to thank Maurice and the team at Maurice Wylie Media for the privilege of being involved in this book project. I have found it challenging and humbling.

Above all, I thank the Lord God for His help. His patience, His unfailing love, His power and His compassion have made all the difference in the lives of people who suffered at the hands of "wicked men". Without the LORD, where would any of us be in our lives? This book celebrates that faith in the Lord Jesus Christ can make a difference in how we live and triumph over suffering. We thank you LORD for who You are and how You have revealed Yourself in the Lord Jesus and how You make Your word and Your presence real by the person of the Holy Spirit.

Pastor Marcus Thomas

Introduction

*"Blessed are those who mourn
for they will be comforted ...
Blessed are the peacemakers, for
they will be called sons of God."*
Matthew 5:4,9.

"Not another book on the Troubles?", I can hear people say. "Let's move on," would be the opinion of some; "There have been enough written and published already." I agree. There is a plethora of material out there about this dark period in the history of Great Britain and Northern Ireland. In writing this book I certainly didn't want to "re-invent the wheel" or just reshape material that is readily available.

The focus of this book is the Christian and the Troubles and, in my research, I discovered that a book had already been published in 2019 around the same theme.

It is called "Considering Grace: Presbyterians and the Troubles."[1] The back cover gives this introduction to the book; "Considering Grace records the deeply moving stories of 120 ordinary people's experiences of the Troubles, exploring how faith shaped their responses to violence and its aftermath."

---

[1] Ganiel G. and Yohanis J. (2019) "Considering Grace: Presbyterians and the Troubles". Ireland, Merrion Press.

Here also, I want to explore the stories of people who suffered in the Troubles but found their faith in Jesus Christ to be the help and strength they needed to carry on. These people have gone through many dark days and nights. They are still going through such periods. There have been times of desperation, tears and heartache but faith has been their comfort, hope and light in the darkness.

However, there is something else which I have endeavored to weave into this book. I fear that the Bible message of suffering is missing from many pulpits and sermons today. There seem to be plenty of motivational statements and "feel good" catch phrases, but are these sufficient when suffering, tests and trials come? The reasons for suffering experiences in our lives can be many.

John Stott wrote, "The fact of suffering undoubtedly constitutes the single greatest challenge to the Christian faith, and has been in every generation. Its distribution and degree appear to be entirely random and therefore unfair." [2]

I had a Christian colleague who had multiple-sclerosis for over 30 years. This medical condition robbed him of many positive things in life. He died recently. I remember him talking to me about the day a doctor told him, "Pastor, you have multiple-sclerosis." He never gave in to the condition but, with great courage and resilience, continued to serve the Lord. He became the lead player in the re-establishing of a Bible School. He studied for a doctorate. But he lived with this medical condition which had no cure.

We are familiar with the saying, "Bad things happen to good people." We find this sobering verse in Ecclesiastes 7:15, *"I have seen everything during my lifetime of futility; there is a righteous man who perishes in*

---

2   Stott, J. (1989), "The Cross of Christ", Leicester, Inter-Varsity Fellowship.

his righteousness and there is a wicked man who prolongs his life in his wickedness." (NASB) I found this comment on Ecclesiastes 7:15:

> *"The situation in verse 15 is a paradox, an irregularity from the way one would expect a thing to be. A paradox is an inconsistency in circumstance, statement, activity, or conduct contrary to what a person would consider normal. Here, the paradox is found within a relationship with God. The sinner prospers, but the righteous suffers all kinds of difficulty in life. Is it not more natural to think that the sinner would have difficulty and the righteous, a prosperous, smooth-running life?"*

A paradox, in turn, creates a conundrum, that is, a riddle or puzzle. A righteous individual may ask, 'Why should such a situation exist?' 'Where are the blessings God has promised?' 'Where is God in this picture?' 'Has God not promised prosperity and long life if we obey Him?' Yes, He has."[3]

Jesus said, *"In this world you will have trouble. But take heart! I have overcome the world."* John 16:33. What is Jesus saying to us in these words? Is he saying that suffering can be a means of knowing him is a deeper way?

There are many stories in the Bible about people who suffered. Some suffered as a consequence of their own actions and attitudes and God brought judgement to their lives. However, the story of Job provides a different perspective. He is described as a man who was *"blameless and upright; he feared God and shunned evil."* Job 1:1. We know what happened. He lost his children, his servants and his herds. The last verse of chapter 1 states, *"In all this, Job did not sin by charging God with wrongdoing."* Job1:22. He then suffers an acute and isolating, physical illness from *"painful sores from the soles of his feet to the top*

---

3 Theberean.org

of his head." Job 2:7. Job's wife challenged him to curse God, but his answer was, *"'Shall we accept good from God, and not trouble?' In all this Job did not sin in what he said."* Job 2:10.

One of the most horrific incidents of the Troubles was the shooting at a Pentecostal church in Darkley, South Armagh. Three elders were killed and members of the congregation were injured. This indiscriminate and unprovoked attack brought condemnation from around the world. The son of one of the three church elders who were murdered, Rodney Wilson, tells his story in chapter 3. A Northern Ireland news correspondent had the privilege of sitting down with one of the widows just eighteen hours after the fatal attack. The reporter writes, "As she (Mrs Elizabeth Brown) delivered the tea to me I said… that she really shouldn't worry about me at a time of such grief for her. 'But we are not grieving, son,' she replied.' 'We are rejoicing that Harold (her husband) is with the Redeemer right now. You see Harold was ready to be with the Lord as all the people were in that hall.' Then she smiled and said, 'You see, I know where he is right now.'" [4]

Norah Bradford, whose husband Robert was murdered by the Irish Republican Army (IRA)[5], writes this about her experience of handling this tragedy as a Christian: "The generations that come after me will have a freer passage if I walk a Godly way forward and find a way to navigate the pain from the horror of sleepless nights and the flashbacks of killing scenes. To find the joy of the Lord and His freedom is a deliberate road and one I had to pursue, regardless of the pulls of pain to keep me in the past. Yes, the path to freedom is full of potholes, ditches of anger, and fury that I frequently fall

---

[4] Henderson D. and Little I. (2018), "Reporting the Troubles". Newtownards, The Blackstaff Press.

[5] Irish Republican Army (IRA) (also called the Provisional Irish Republican Army) – a Republican paramilitary organization seeking the establishment of a republic, the end of British rule in Northern Ireland, and the reunification of Ireland. (Britannica).

into, but I crawl out, shake myself off (many times just me and the Lord) and move on."[6]

In this book you will find stories of faith from Northern Ireland. Also, I trust, you will learn about the place of suffering in the Christian life and how it can transform your heart.

Peter writes, *"In this you greatly rejoice, though now for a little while you may have had to suffer grief in all kinds of trials. These have come so that your faith – of greater worth than gold, which perishes even though refined by fire – may be proved genuine and may result in praise, glory and honor when Jesus Christ is revealed."* 1 Peter 1:6-7.

In all our suffering, as Christians, we have not only the teaching of Jesus on suffering, but also His example, in what He suffered, as Peter says, *"by the hands of lawless and wicked men."* Acts 2:23 (AMP)

John Stott wrote, "For Jesus spoke of suffering as being both 'for God's glory', that God's Son might be glorified through it, and 'so that the work of God might be displayed'."[7] John 9:3 and 11:4. That has certainly happened through Jesus' sufferings and death on the Cross. But we must remember the cost of his death, emotionally, physically and spiritually before His Father in heaven. The pain, the agony, the abandonment, the undeserved punishment through the nails, the curses and mocking of men and the vulnerability of being on a cross, open to the elements of the day was a terrible way to die. This was all according to the purpose of Jesus being our Suffering Saviour. He didn't retaliate, He didn't call for angels to help him escape, He didn't curse His Father, but *"as a sheep before its shearers is silent, so He did not open his mouth."* Isaiah 53:7. He has left us his words and His example regarding suffering. He suffered for being

---

[6] Bradford N. (2021), "When Time Is Taken", Belfast, Maurice Wylie Media.
[7] Stott, J. (1989), "The Cross of Christ", Leicester, Inter-Varsity Fellowship.

good and doing good. He suffered as someone who had never sinned in word, thought or deed. And it was for the glory of God, His Father. The writer of Hebrews tells us:

> *"Let us fix our eyes on Jesus, the author and perfecter of our faith, who for the joy set before Him endured the cross, scorning its shame... consider Him who endured such opposition from sinful men, so that you will not grow weary and lose heart."* Hebrews 12:2-3.

I don't intend this book to give glib and cheap answers to suffering or to lay out a process for people to follow in handling the tests and the trials that come to Christian lives. Instead, I want to delve into the promises that God has made to people who suffer and the guidelines that He has laid down as to how we should respond to such heartaches. In doing so, I trust the following chapters will illustrate how those promises and guidelines have become a reality for the individuals whose stories you will read.

A Biblical example of this is the familiar, Old Testament story of Ruth. Although she was a Gentile, she came back to Israel, with Naomi her Jewish mother-in-law, as a worshipper of Jehovah. Both were widows. Naomi was mourning her misfortune that she had left Israel full of possessions and blessings but was coming back empty, with no husband and no sons. However, the LORD had laid down in the nation of Israel principles and guidelines to help people in such situations. The thrill of the story is this: through God arranged "coincidences" and the obedience of a relative, God's word became real and brought Ruth and Naomi from a place of emptiness to a place of fullness. God's Word worked for these two sorrowing widows.

There is much written in the Bible about God's comfort and help for us in our sufferings and trials and tests. The question is: will it and does it work in the 21st century? Through the stories included in this book, I trust you will experience both encouragement and strength from realising that God is with us in "the valley of the shadow of death" and He does prepare "a table in the wilderness." His Word and His promises do work and will bring comfort and guidance for us in all our tests and trials.

The Troubles

"This Man, when handed over [to the Roman authorities] according to the predetermined decision and foreknowledge of God, you nailed to a cross and put to death by the hands of lawless and godless men."
Acts 2:23 (AMP)

The years of the Troubles in Northern Ireland were some of the bleakest and saddest years in our nation's history. They lasted from 1968 to 1998 and their impact overflowed to mainland Britain and endures, even to the present day. A civil rights rally in Londonderry in October 1968 ignited a spark that brought sickening scenes of violence to the streets of Northern Ireland and beyond. Wicked, godless and lawless individuals walked the streets carrying out an evil campaign of violence. There were targeted murders and bomb attacks. There were tit-for-tat killings. Many innocent individuals were killed because they were in the wrong place at the wrong time and were caught in the crossfire.

Varying figures exist about the numbers of dead and injured as a result of these years of mayhem and bloodshed. One report states, "In a small community like Northern Ireland, the murder of 3,500 people and the maiming of almost 40,000 citizens has an impact in almost every home. If those statistics were taken in proportion to the population of the USA more than 650,000 people would have been killed and 7.5 million people maimed."[8] Another document records that over 100,000 were injured, 37,000 shootings and over 16,000 bombing attacks. However, elsewhere it was reported: "Exact figures for the toll of the terrorist campaign are impossible to come by."[9]

The reality of the Troubles cannot be left to a set of statistics. Behind the figures for those murdered or maimed, both physically and emotionally, are families: mothers, fathers, husbands, wives, children, brothers, sisters, grandparents, aunts and uncles, cousins and neighbours. I wondered how many tears were shed and are still shed for lost family members and friends.

"The Troubles were a tragedy that unfolded over three long decades of violence and destruction. Countless individuals … suffered emotional trauma and post-traumatic stress. The impact of these traumas rippled out to family and friends, impacting the whole of society, to varying degrees."[10]

David McKittrick, an author and journalist, wrote, "Those who died in the Troubles included civilians, members of loyalist and republican groups, political figures, soldiers, joyriders, alleged drug dealers, judges and magistrates, those killed during armed robberies, prison officers, police officers, convicted killers, businessmen, alleged informers, military personal, those who died on hunger strike, men, women, children, pensioners and unborn babies."[11]

The heartache, the sleepless nights, the anger, the pain, the suffering that these years brought to many, many people can never be fully estimated. It's impossible to put a cost on the emotional and mental

---

8   Bradford N. (2021), "When Time Is Taken", Belfast, Maurice Wylie Media.
9   Henderson D. and Little I. (2018), "Reporting the Troubles 1". Newtownards, The Blackstaff Press.
10 Ganiel G. and Yohanis J. (2019) "Considering Grace: Presbyterians and the Troubles". Ireland, Merrion Press.
11 Henderson D. and Little I. (2018), "Reporting the Troubles 1". Newtownards, The Blackstaff Press.

torment that families suffered during those thirty years. Although there was an agreement in 1998 between all sides involved in the Troubles, the pain, the suffering and the mental scars of those years are still very real for many, many people. They were left with only their memories and photographs of the friends and family members that were killed and our hearts go out to them.

While recognizing that some individuals are still living with the historical trauma, there are some people who, through their faith, have come to a place of healing. It has taken some years to find this place of healing. The memories of what happened to them will never go away, but, by the grace of God and the praying support of Christian friends, family and their local church, there are those who have come to a place of peace.

Stories from the Troubles…

McKittrick in the book, "Reporting the Troubles 1", mentions the heartbreaking story of James Seymour: "There are many heart-rending tales…There is, for example, the story of Royal Ulster Constabulary constable James Seymour who was shot in 1973 and for twenty-two years lay in a hospital bed, a bullet in his head, apparently conscious but unable to move or speak. On every day of those twenty-two years, he was visited by his wife. He died at the age of fifty-five in 1995, bringing the vigil of two decades to a close: the strain and anguish suffered by him and his family can only be imagined. Many families have found that such scars may never heal. Although the Seymour family suffered particularly severely, their protracted, heartbreaking tragedy is only one of hundreds arising from a quarter-century of death and destruction, affecting many types of people. Among the wounded are many in wheelchairs or confined to bed, or who have brain damage. Some are in constant pain."[12]

---

12 Henderson D. and Little I. (2018), "Reporting the Troubles 1". Newtownards, The Blackstaff Press.

In the book "Considering Grace" there is a story about a person called Edna. Her husband was killed in a bomb attack on an army barracks. Edna, we are told, "turned to alcohol to deal with the pain." She said, "I took a sleeping tablet and half a glass of whiskey every night going to bed."[13] She did stop this practice and has gone on to find some solace in faith but admits she still finds the memories of what happened a struggle, especially when the anniversary of her husband's death comes around.

Norah Bradford, whose husband, Robert Bradford MP, was murdered on November 14th, 1981, wrote: "It has taken me the full 40 years to come out of the hurt, pain, anguish, betrayal, deception and every other emotion that goes with the territory of having a loved one snatched from the family, never in this world to be held again. My love for the Lord means I know Robert's safe and can't be harmed any further and, in fact, is happier than he's ever been, living, smiling and laughing in the beautiful place called Heaven, totally present with his King."[14]

In the book "Fire on the Mountain"[15] we read something of the story of Esther Wilson. Her father was David Wilson and he was murdered, along with two other men, when terrorists attacked a Pentecostal church near Keady. Esther writes, "Grieving the loss of my father, friend and mentor did not come easily. As a family, our way of processing grief was to not talk about it. It wasn't until 15 years later that a long deep process of healing and grieving would begin. This process was the key that would unlock the empty dark place in my heart that I'd put the lid on so many years earlier, watching my dad being buried … Healing does not happen in isolation. I have learned by experience that real healing takes time. It occurs only in

---

13 Ganiel G. and Yohanis J. (2019) "Considering Grace: Presbyterians and the Troubles". Ireland, Merrion Press.
14 Bradford N. (2021), "When Time Is Taken", Belfast, Maurice Wylie Media.
15 Bell D. (2013) "Fire on the Mountain", Belfast, Ambassador Books and Media.

a place where God's presence, God's peace and God's people are. God promises in Jeremiah 29:11, 'I know the plans I have for you … plans to prosper and not to harm you, plans to give you hope and a future.' Although there will be times in our life when these words seem impossible to reconcile with our grief, God does have a plan for us, and we do indeed have a future and a hope."

The Troubles brought a complete change of culture in Northern Ireland and, this change also spread across to the mainland. People were on high alert and living in fear: where would the next attack take place? Who would be the next target? What tit-for-tat reprisals would hit the headlines?

Belfast during the Troubles…

Shauneen Armstrong, who lived in Belfast, remembers, "Once while in school we heard a bomb go off and the teacher stopped the class and asked us to pray that no one would be hurt. As we were praying, we realised the teacher was crying and being 11 or 12 years old, we were shocked, embarrassed and did not know what to do. She told us how she was so sad for us because being born in the early 1970s, we never knew the wonderful Belfast before the Troubles. That was something we heard a lot growing up. When in town, it was normal to go into a security cabin to be searched. How, after that, you'd be searched going in and out of every shop."[16] Shauneen, when talking about her experiences through Twitter had a reply from someone who had also lived in Northern Ireland during the Troubles. This person remembered going to a shopping mall while on holiday in America and stopping at the security guard to hold up their arms and be searched. The security guard thought she wanted a hug. Shauneen writes, "It was a habitual routine you did without thinking."

---

16 Armstrong S. (2018), "Growing up in the Troubles", thejournal.ie.

In Belfast buses, taxis and cars were hijacked; businesses firebombed; school hours disrupted or suspended for the safety of the children and checkpoints set up by the army or terrorist groups to both monitor and stop attacks on their communities. For anybody travelling into Belfast by car for work, they would often have to find alternative routes to get there and return home because of rioting or incidents on the streets, which would then mean going through a checkpoint, where their car may have been hijacked by a terrorist group.

On the BBC website there is an article headed, "The Troubles: When Belfast children fled the city." It starts with this introduction, "In the early years of the Troubles, as sectarian violence flared across Northern Ireland, thousands of people fled their homes. Some were burnt out, others had windows broken or faced intimidation, some feared for their lives but many others just needed a break from the constant stress of violence in their neighbourhood. The vast majority of people returned to their homes, many in a few weeks, but others never came back."[17]

The following statement appears in the article: "The outbreak of sectarian violence in Northern Ireland during the late summer of 1969 'gave rise to a refugee crisis which at the time, represented the largest involuntary movement of population in Europe since the end of World War Two." (Dr Niall Gilmartin). Perhaps this statement is now outdated with the exodus we have seen from the Ukraine, but it does highlight the danger and fear that people were living under to attempt to escape from the city of Belfast. A particular feature of the refugee crisis in Belfast was the evacuation of children to parts of Ireland, Scotland and England.

"BBC journalists reported on the evacuation of 1971 on both sides of the community. Nationwide reporter Philip Tibenham travelled

---

17 Sheeran R. (2021), "The Troubles: When Belfast children fled the city". BBC, N. Ireland.

to Scotland by ferry with a group of mothers and children from the Crumlin Road area of north Belfast. One Protestant mother he spoke to says her child has been on the barbiturate drug phenobarbitone for months to help her sleep. 'These children are in a war of nerves just like us mothers,' said another. Literally only a few places away from where these children live are Roman Catholic kids who are going through the same nightmare, The BBC journalist concludes."

The Border and South Armagh during the Troubles...

In South Armagh, and other counties along the border, the republican paramilitary groups had an "ethnic cleansing policy".

In a book called "Ireland's Violent Border" the writer, Professor Henry Patterson told this story of "Douglas Deering, the last Protestant shopkeeper in Roslea, close to the border in Fermanagh. He was a married man with three children and a devout Christian who attended a gospel hall across the border in Clones. His shop was bombed four times and then, eventually, he was shot dead in the premises on May 12, 1977."

Another story comes from John Devine, former Northern Editor of the Irish Independent. He writes, "The old man sobbed uncontrollably for over ten minutes, occasionally wailing. Broken, beyond words. Stripped of all dignity. Unforgettable.

He had been recounting for me how his inheriting son, who worked part-time on the farm, had been murdered just two weeks after it had been signed over to him. To use the parlance of the day, what I was researching was really 'the murder of Prods on the border'. The words 'ethnic cleansing' had not yet entered the lexicon of everyday usage.

Irish border Protestants believed that the IRA plan was to have fewer of them and more Catholic landowners there, and a more porous frontier."

To escape these IRA threats some of the Protestant farmers went to Scotland. Others moved to nearby towns but still worked their farms.

Devine continues, "Often when working the land, or tending animals, the womenfolk would ride tractor shotgun for their menfolk. But not all the men had women. The bachelors were easy pickings for the assassins. And not all women either were exempt from being murdered."[18]

The farmer told John Devine that "two men dressed in boiler suits came into the farmyard, unseen. His wife heard the shots and found the son slumped over the tractor steering wheel. She saw the killers disappear across the field behind the house, heading for the border and in no great hurry."

The only person that the farmer had spoken to about the handover was a Catholic neighbour. They were friends and had known each other for years. They had relied on each other for help and support during the ups and the downs of the farming year. Their families grew up together.

The farmer said, "Perhaps over the dinner table, my friend, as part of normal daily chat, mentioned that I had signed over the farm. It had never crossed my mind before that not all his family would have his views, or his loyalty. I just assumed that when I spoke to him, things would go no further. I now know that not to be true. I know also I can never confide in him again."

---

18   Henderson D. and Little I. (2018), "Reporting the Troubles 1". Newtownards, The Blackstaff Press.

An article appeared in the Newsletter[19] on July 5th, 2016, with this headline –

"Victim opens up on how IRA ethnic cleansing gang targeted his home."

The article continued with the story: (name of the IRA commander removed)

> "I was only 15," he said. "My father was coming home from work and the boys (IRA) were sitting in our lane waiting for him. They walked him in at gunpoint."
>
> He and his 10-year-old sister went out to meet his father as normal – he usually had sweets for them.
>
> "We met him in our lane with six gunmen with him – all masked. They said to us, 'If you run, we will shoot you', so we walked in with them. They had a gun stuck at dad's back." In those days the IRA launched attacks on the same day every week. His father used to say: "I wonder who is going to be shot this Thursday?"
>
> They took the family hostage for two hours, waiting for his brother – a part-time Ulster Defence Regiment (UDR)[20] member – to return. His father protested as they ransacked the house and the leader shouted: "You shut your mouth." The IRA man stuck the gun into his father's mouth.
>
> Although masked, the family knew it was local IRA commander ▮▮▮▮▮▮▮▮▮▮ as he had only one hand – he lost the other

---

19 Newsletter – Belfast daily newspaper.
20 The Ulster Defence Regiment (UDR) was an infantry regiment of the British Army established in 1970, with a comparatively short existence ending in 1992. (Wikipedia).

in a premature bomb. My mammy said 'Don't be shooting him – he is the only one to look after us'. ▇▇▇ replied: 'Well we will shoot the boy instead, Maybe, this boy is in the UDR too.'

Then he started to beat me with the butt of his gun and started kicking me. His mother lay on him to protect him. He went on: "▇▇▇ said: 'Don't you worry. You are going to be out of this part of the country.' My father replied: 'No way will I be moving.' They took UDR uniforms and smashed every light and every piece of furniture we had.

As they left, the IRA gang saw a car coming round the corner which appeared to be the brother's car. They opened fire and the driver was killed – however it turned out to be an elderly neighbour.

His parents suffered depression, strokes and heart disease. He himself suffered a heart attack at 37. 'It was all stress-related. Nobody knows the pressure we were under. 'They came back and shot the house up a year later. Our neighbour got his throat cut. 'People kept well out of the road. They did not travel at night. They only left the house to worship or get groceries. We were not free to do what we wanted. It was awful.

'Now I still have mental health problems – and they tell me I am fit to work. They should leave victims like us to live in peace with pensions."

These three stories highlight the policy of "ethnic cleansing" that the IRA followed in South Armagh and the other border areas of Northern Ireland.

There were personal attacks, but the infrastructure, the cultural life and the atmosphere of these border areas were affected.[21]

- Many border roads were closed, which impacted the daily lives of people. "The closure of most border roads during the Troubles dramatically impacted on the everyday lives of people living near the border. For people whose journeys to work, church, school, to shop, or to visit family or friends were affected by road closures ..."

- Some roads were blocked or cratered. "Those living on roads that ended at a crater at the border experienced not only the serious inconvenience of no longer being able to travel in that direction but the strangeness of being isolated and restricted in this way."

- The checkpoints caused delay and some people, who worked across the border, would try to find alternative routes to avoid the delays. Not all the checkpoints were set up by the British army. Someone wrote, "You never knew where you were going to find the road blocked or who blocked it ..."

- "The attempt to seal the border depended on a very heavy military presence along the border in Northern Ireland. Army patrols and checkpoints responded to IRA violence in the borderlands and provoked attack. Army checkpoints, The Royal Ulster Constabulary (RUC)[22] police stations and army and RUC patrols were targeted by the IRA. Members of the RUC or UDR were targeted in shootings. Catholics that were judged by the IRA as being in collaboration with the security forces, and Protestants with no connection to the security forces were also murdered."

---

21 "The Troubles and borderland life." irishborderlands.com
22 The Royal Ulster Constabulary (RUC) was the police force in Northern Ireland from 1922 to 2001. It was founded on 1 June 1922 as a successor to the Royal Irish Constabulary (RIC) following the partition of Ireland. At its peak the force had around 8,500 officers, with a further 4,500 who were members of the RUC Reserve. (Wikipedia).

This heavy military presence on the border brought, for some, fear, anxiety and terror to their community. But for others this presence was reassuring. "Many who were not directly in contact with the security forces lived with a sense of being under constant surveillance especially in the areas of South Armagh and Tyrone where British army watchtowers were built along the hills near the border and where the sight and sound of army helicopters were part of everyday life."

"As in other parts of Northern Ireland, violent incidents and the fear and suspicion they created deeply damaged previously warm or at best politely friendly relationships between Catholics and Protestants in the borderlands. Patterns of collective support amongst communities of small farmers, Protestant and Catholic – helping at harvest, sharing machinery, helping in times of need – were destroyed. The strangeness of local UDR men formally asking their neighbours their names and address as a requirement of their duties estranged people from each other."

It was Merlyn Rees, former Secretary of State for Northern Ireland, in the 1970's who called South Armagh "Bandit Country". The title was given because the area was a known IRA stronghold. It was "one of the most dangerous and unforgiving places on earth for British soldiers and other security force personnel during the 30 year "conflict" and the South Armagh IRA seemed able to slaughter at will and the area's nickname, 'Bandit Country', was written in the blood of the innocent."[23] So, South Armagh was a place that required a strong military presence.

"The South Armagh Brigade of the Provisional Irish Republican Army (IRA) operated during the Troubles in south County Armagh. It was organised into two battalions, one around Jonesborough and another around Crossmaglen. By the 1990s, the South Armagh Brigade was

---

23 See belfastchildis.com

thought to consist of about 40 members, roughly half of them living south of the border.

As well as paramilitary activity, the South Armagh Brigade has also been widely accused of smuggling across the Irish border. Other activities included money-laundering and fraud through embezzlement of agricultural subsidies and false claims of property loss. Some sources claim that the smuggling activities not only made the South Armagh brigade self-sufficient, but also provided financial support to most of the IRA operations around Northern Ireland. The IRA control over the roads across the border in South Armagh enabled them to impose duty on every cross-border illegal enterprise.

Between 1970 and 1997 the brigade was responsible for the deaths of 165 members of the British security forces (123 British soldiers and 42 RUC officers). A further 75 civilians were killed in the area during the conflict, as well as ten South Armagh Brigade members. The RUC recorded 1,255 bombings and 1,158 shootings around a radius of ten miles from the geographic centre of South Armagh in the same period."[24]

What about the loyalist paramilitary organisations? There are two particular groups we need to mention:

Firstly, there was a group in Armagh linked to the Mid-Ulster Brigade, which was part of the Ulster Volunteer Force (UVF)[25]. "The brigade was established in Lurgan, County Armagh in 1972 and carried out many attacks, mainly in Northern Ireland, especially in the South Armagh area, but it also extended its operational reach into the Republic of Ireland. Two of the most notorious attacks in the history of the Troubles were carried out by the Mid-Ulster Brigade: the

---

24 Source – Wikipedia.
25 The Ulster Volunteer Force (UVF) is an Ulster loyalist paramilitary group. Formed in 1965,[7] it first emerged in 1966. Its first leader was Gusty Spence, a former British Army soldier from Northern Ireland. (deleted the name: Wikipedia)

1974 Dublin and Monaghan bombings[26] and the Miami Showband killings in 1975[27]."

Secondly, there was a group called the Glenanne Gang: "The Glenanne gang or Glenanne group was a secret informal alliance of Ulster loyalists who carried out shooting and bombing attacks against Catholics and Irish nationalists in the 1970s, during the Troubles. Most of its attacks took place in the "murder triangle" area of counties Armagh and Tyrone in Northern Ireland. It also launched some attacks elsewhere in Northern Ireland and in the Republic of Ireland."[28]

This gang included members from the UVF and the British law and enforcement services in Northern Ireland. They were a clandestine and shadowy group. Their activities in past years have been thoroughly investigated and the conclusion has been that there was collusion between this group and the British military and Secret Services and the police. A book, "Lethal Allies", focusing on the activities of the Glenanne gang was published in 2013. It estimated that the group killed about 120 people. Nearly all of them were Catholic civilians with no links to republican paramilitaries.

I can remember, quite soon after we moved to live in Northern Ireland in 1999, hearing about "Bandit country". What must it have been like to live in this area of South Armagh – living with the fear of what news a day would bring or hearing of the murder of a friend or family

---

26 Dublin and Monaghan bombings. On 17th May 1974 three car bombs exploded in Dublin city centre killing 26 people and injuring nearly 300 people. Ninety minutes after the three Dublin blasts, a fourth car bomb went off in Monaghan. Seven people were killed. No warnings were given for these attacks which brought about the greatest loss of life in a single day in the history of the Troubles.

27 Miami Showband killings. The showband was returning to Dublin on 31 July at about 2.30 a.m. after a performance in Banbridge. They were flagged down at a bogus vehicle checkpoint on a road near Newry by armed members of the Mid-Ulster Brigade wearing British Army uniforms. This attack went wrong. Three band members were killed and another two were injured. Two members of the brigade were also killed.

28 Source – Wikipedia

member? What about the individuals who had already suffered? What was it like for them when they heard about another killing or bombing? I would have visited many times the Mountain Lodge Pentecostal church, where three elders were shot dead. The wooden building that was sprayed with bullets is still standing, alongside a new church building. Although it had happened many years prior to our coming to live in County Armagh, on every visit that barbaric incident, with its pain and sorrow, would come to mind.

"Bandit country"! What a label for the place where you were born and lived! People there felt vulnerable, afraid of being caught in the crossfire or being in the wrong place at the wrong time. The atmosphere of suspicion was palpable. Distrust, tension and fear of revenge, were the order of these dreadful times in South Armagh. The southern part of the county was extensively militarized, with the heavy presence of the British army and the paramilitary groups at war with each other. Communities were divided and friendships spoilt forever.

Personal memories...

I spent the years of the Troubles living in various parts of the UK, so most of my experience was at a distance. My information and knowledge came from watching TV news and documentaries and reading newspapers. Looking back, certain incidents still stand out in my mind. The Enniskillen bombing, in County Fermanagh, which killed eleven people in November 1987, is one memory. The dignity and the generosity of Gordon Wilson, who lost a daughter, really impacted me. I remember also the vivid and dramatic pictures on the TV of Michael Stone fleeing the scene of his attack on a funeral at Milltown Cemetery, West Belfast, in March 1988.

At the beginning, the Troubles were contained within Northern Ireland, but later they spread across to the mainland. Two young boys were killed in the Warrington bombing in March 1993. I can still remember the grief of one of the fathers who had lost his precious, only son. In October 1984, an IRA bomb exploded at the Conservative party conference in Brighton. From news coverage, I vividly recall seeing the victims emerge from the scene dishevelled, with cuts to their faces and covered in dust.

However, in June 1996 the Troubles came very close to us as a family. An IRA bomb exploded in Manchester city centre, very close to the music school where our thirteen-year-old, middle daughter was boarding. It was a 1,500- kilogram lorry bomb – the biggest bomb detonated in the UK since the Second World War. We were living in the Highlands of Scotland at the time and were away in Perth at a Christian conference. We didn't have a mobile in those days and it was only when we arrived home, late in the evening, that we learned what had happened. The school suffered many broken windows and a cello was split in two with flying glass, but, by the grace of God, no pupil suffered life-threatening injuries. Our daughter had glass removed from her eye and was taken home by one of her teachers, badly shaken and very upset. For some time after the incident, whenever she heard an alarm go off, it would bring back the panic of that day.

Living in Northern Ireland…

In July 1999 we moved, as a family, to live in Lurgan, a town in North Armagh, where we remained for 19 years. About six weeks before we moved over permanently, we went to Northern Ireland to view the church manse. I can remember the shock we felt on seeing armed soldiers walking both sides of a main road into the town. The car went quiet. In the 19 years we lived and served the LORD in North Armagh, we never experienced any of the incidents that took place even after the Agreement in 1998. However, what I did become aware of was the legacy of the Troubles in the local community.

Visiting the home of a church member, in my early days, I was shown a rubber bullet. It was a large rubber baton of the type used frequently during the Troubles, constructed with a solid metal core and many times bigger than a conventional bullet. These rubber bullets had a significant impact on anyone they hit. The man who showed me the bullet expressed his anger and sense of betrayal that the British army had fired these bullets at loyalists who, in his view, were "only defending their country".

There was a woman in the congregation whose twin brother had been shot dead in the town by mistake. People spoke well of him and he attended a Christian church in the town and was engaged to be married. His grieving fiancée never married.

She was not the only member of the congregation affected. A second woman also had a brother shot dead. He was a serving policeman. She was still very hurt and it was heartbreaking to hear her talk about the loss of her brother. A third had a son who was very badly wounded in an incident and carried his injuries for the rest of his life. He eventually left the town to live overseas and found it very difficult to come back to Northern Ireland to visit his family.

Memories from friends…

I spoke with some friends of mine, who lived and worked in Northern Ireland during the Troubles, asking them to write something about their experiences. The first two friends are both called John.

John's story… (1)

"My name is John and I was in my teens when the Troubles began. Although they never directly affected our family, I remember the constant coverage and debate on the TV. I heard my father and grandfather, on a regular basis in the home, discussing the issues and the events surrounding this sad time in our history.

My life was not dictated by the Troubles, though I do remember walking round the City Hall looking for an exit route to great Victoria Street Station as bombs went off around us. I also remember walking home to Suffolk from Central Belfast, with my wife May, as all buses had been cancelled due to bomb scares and street unrest.

Later I remember working on the Springfield Road when a rocket was fired at the Police and army barracks, that made a rather large noise on impact. The Troubles were noted and worked around.

I accepted the rule of law as per the Bible, that government was put in place by God, and refused to accept the right to bear arms by either side and acted as the security forces required.

No one from my immediate family was injured or murdered but a neighbour of ours was killed on the Chinook,[29] that crashed on the hillside in Scotland. It had a terrible effect on his wife and 3 young children."

John's story... (2)

"My name is John. As the Troubles were starting in 1970, I was thirteen. I attended the Royal Belfast Academical Institution which is located in the centre of Belfast. So, I went to school at

---

29 June 2nd, 1994, an RAF Chinook helicopter crashed into a mountain on the Mull of Kintyre. 29 people were killed.

the height of the IRA bombing campaign. On two occasions I had to walk home because the bus service had been suspended because of bombings.

Because of the dangers from terrorists, teenage activities were very much curtailed during this period. There was always the threat of getting caught up in a terrorist incident.

Also, my father was a RUC officer. Much of the danger he faced we took as a way of life. Thankfully, he was never injured, or worse, killed. Yet, no doubt, the threat was always there. Some of his friends, however, were not so fortunate.

Not only was I entering my teenage years, and attending school in the most bombed city in Europe, but it was also about this time I had an encounter with the Lord that transformed my life — I met Jesus Christ. While this was so important to me, I didn't really make the connection between what was happening in the country and what was happening in my own life. Later on, I realised my faith played a big part in bringing me through this turbulent period in our history.

My faith also helped me later on, when I experienced the call of God on my life to full-time ministry. As I have ministered to people who have lost ones through the Troubles, my faith in Jesus has been absolutely essential in being able to help others through a very difficult experience.

As always, things look a lot clearer. I can now see what a divine intervention took place in my life when I encountered Christ."

Neil's story...

Growing up in Northern Ireland during the Troubles was filled with both joy and sorrow. For as long as I can mind, the noise of helicopters, police sirens and army Land Rovers was part of my life – not to mention the bombs and the shootings.

Each day the news would report of yet another man or woman killed. One day would be a loyalist, the next day a nationalist and so the cycle would go. The world into which I was born was one of a strong community and one of total chaos. As young Protestants in Northern Ireland, we had a saying that brought us both strength and comfort. The saying was, 'For God and Ulster' It seems strange now, but I, and many like me, believed wholeheartedly, that God really was on the side of the Loyalists.

Growing up as a young boy among so much death and destruction can harden the heart and numb the senses. An example of this can be found in what I experienced as a young boy aged thirteen.

On May 13th, 1991 as I made my way to school, I witnessed first-hand a car bomb that left a man trapped inside his mangled car burning to death. Up until this point in my life bombs had made a lot of noise and left a lot of destruction but they didn't affect me the way this affected me – the reason being, I saw this first hand, not on a TV. As I said before, death was common – even expected. But this was different. My own eyes witnessed this great evil.

I recall what appeared to be a man's hands reaching up among the smoke and flames, as if trying to escape from this burning twisted car. To be told about a man or woman being murdered is one thing. But to witness it is something very different. I continued to make my way to school. On arrival, all pupils were called to gather in the assembly hall and the teachers tried to make sure that nobody was caught up in what had just happened. I recall their faces. Many were distraught, horrified. Some children were crying. There was one girl who believed it was her father who was in the car. She was standing there as white as white could be, in total shock.

From that day on, my heart became a little harder and it numbed the senses. What I experienced that day left me both cold and confused as to what life was all about. If there was a God, where was He? My heart was filled with hatred and all I could see was them and us. Through it all I believed that God was on our side. But at the age of twenty-four I heard the Gospel of Jesus Christ – how He came to bring peace and reconcile men to God, to restore that brokenness, that chaos in our lives. I surrendered my life to Him and out of the chaos came joy. My hard heart was made new. My senses that could no longer feel pain began to feel emotion again.

So out of the chaos and destruction came beauty. A new man was born in Christ. Not only did I find a new love for God, but I found a new love for those I once hated. Although my world was filled with darkness, God was in it, for in our war-stricken land the gospel was preached in every corner and a great light shone in the heart of our land – a light that led many home to God.

I am saved now 20 years and my father is saved nearly 30. My father and I would often reminisce and talk about the past. One thing that seems to be very clear to me regarding my father is that God appeared to be with him from a young age. Now it must be said, that many a young man and woman died too soon, and many without Christ. But it can't be denied, God had His hand on my father's life…

In 1984, a very close friend and work colleague of my father was murdered at the age of thirty-seven. My father worked with this man as an undertaker for a few years on the side. His name was Herbie Burrows (see chapter 6 – The Story of Maggie Burrows).

On the March 3, 1984, as Herbie made his way to his premises, as he did every day to prepare for the day's work, he was murdered by a bomb. The door to the premises was broken and wouldn't lock properly, so each day Herbie would kick the door to open it, but this would be the last time he would kick the door to his premises.

That night the IRA had set a booby trap bomb at the door, so when Herbie kicked it the bomb was triggered. Herbie wouldn't have known what hit him. This was a time of great sorrow for my father personally and for the man's family. What my father recalls about that dark day, on the March 3rd, 1984, was that he too was meant to be with Herbie that morning to work but the previous night my father had broken his leg in a football match and was therefore unable to attend his work. His life was spared that day.

I would love to say my father turned to God in fear and thanksgiving but that's not how it went. My father continued to live in his sin and hatred for the other side, as we called them, and made many mistakes outside of Christ. One mistake would lead him to Christ and usher in a freedom that was both spiritual and physical. My father got caught up with paramilitaries and was caught by police while taking part in paramilitary activity. He found himself in a holding cell and about to be imprisoned.

At that moment he got a revelation of the life he had been living. The madness he was born into had got into his head and he, like thousands of others, was being used as an instrument for evil. After a few nights in the cell my father got on his knees before God and cried out to Him. He repented of his sin and made a promise that, if God would somehow get him out of this mess, he would devote the rest of his life to Him (a promise, that by the grace of God he has kept this far).

Today our lives are made new and our hearts are restored. The deep hatred that once burned within us has gone out and a new fire now burns brightly within us – a fire for God and a love for Christ. Our lives in Northern Ireland were sharpened by hatred and fueled by anger. We cried out, 'For God and Ulster! No surrender!'. Now we cry out, 'For God so loved the world, He gave …' No longer do we shout, 'No surrender!', rather, we encourage men and women from all walks of life to come to God in repentance through Christ and surrender their lives to him, so they too can experience the peace, joy and restoration that we and many others like us have found in the Lord Jesus Christ. Amid great darkness, the light of the gospel was clearly seen and heard and countless lives were transformed and souls saved. Sadly, in times of peace God is often forgotten and man's need of Christ is often harder for people to see.

But if God can move in troubled times, I am certain He can move in times of peace."

Robin's story…

Robin and his family lived in Lisburn, County Down. Recalling the bombs going off, he said, "If there were no bombs in a week, it was a good week". He told of the day when the windows of the primary school he was attending shook as the Woodlands Hotel was blown up. Whenever a bomb was detonated the windows of the family home would shake! One day when this happened, they found out later that Moira police station had been bombed and they were feeling the fall-out some 5 miles away.

Robin, at 15 years of age, was asked to join the paramilitary group called the Ulster Defence Association (UDA).[30] He didn't join because, as he said, "His mother and father would have killed him". Many parents lived with the fear of their children being drawn into the conflict by the paramilitary organisations on both sides. Of course, many were recruited.

There was an occasion when a gun was pulled out on Robin in a local Chinese restaurant and he was invited to go outside. He refused, thinking, "If they want to shoot me, then they can do it inside the restaurant". On another occasion, a gang had threatened to come and crush Robin's knees. This was because his girlfriend's previous boyfriend was jealous and had arranged for a gang of men to come and beat Robin up. The local UDA group stopped the attack.

Robin's family had relatives in a town in County Armagh. The paramilitary group that controlled the Protestant areas of Lisburn was the UDA, but the town where the relatives lived was controlled by a different paramilitary group. Robin remembers visiting his relatives on one occasion and a man shouting around the estate, "Wombles, Wombles." The family had no link to the UDA but, anyone from Lisburn went under that nickname and were considered a threat.

Robin's family did experience tragedy. On January 6th, an RUC patrol from Newry observed three men acting suspiciously in Rostrevor, a town in County Down, close to the Irish border.

---

30 The Ulster Defence Association (UDA) is an Ulster loyalist paramilitary[9] group in Northern Ireland. It was formed in September 1971 as an umbrella group for various loyalist groups[10] and undertook an armed campaign of almost twenty-four years as one of the participants of the Troubles.

One officer got out of the police vehicle to check the men out. They were armed members of the IRA and opened fire on the RUC patrol, wounding three officers. They were rushed to Daisy Hill Hospital in Newry where Sergeant Brown, Robin's uncle, and Constable Brian Quinn were pronounced dead.[31]

What can we say about these years of murder, bombings and civil unrest on the streets of Northern Ireland, Great Britain and beyond? What a cost! What sadness! What tears did the LORD God witness from heaven and what cries did the LORD God hear during these years of death and destruction? Someone has asked, "If we put a candle in every home, or farm, on every lane or road or street or field, in every building, public or private, where an atrocity took place in those thirty years of terror, what would the aerial view look like?"

Suffering in the World...

Why is there suffering in this world? I want to answer this question from a Biblical perspective. We will look deeper at this question of suffering in the next chapter but, by way of setting the scene, let's consider two reasons for suffering:

Firstly, the Bible tells us that suffering is an intrusion into this world of ours. God can and does bring good out of suffering but it is the LORD bringing good out of evil. Suffering was not part of the creation that God made. It has come because of the fall of man.

Secondly, suffering results from sin. Nicky Gumbel, from Holy Trinity Brompton, writes, "Individual suffering is often caused by the sin of others. So much suffering is caused by murder, adultery, theft, sexual abuse, unloving parents, reckless or drunken driving,

---

31 Burrows S. "From Partition to Peace". County Armagh Phoenix Group Ltd.

slander, un-kindness or selfishness of one kind or another. Some have estimated that perhaps as much as 95 per cent of the world's suffering can be accounted for in this way."[32]

More often than not, when there is suffering, God is blamed for either his inaction or his absence. I remember the terrible tragedy at Aberfan, in South Wales in October 1966, when a coal tip, above the village, gave way and 116 children and 28 adults were killed. People from the village where I lived, went to Aberfan to help the clearing up operation. An official enquiry followed and it was found that the National Coal Board was responsible for the disaster. "As one woman who contributed to the disaster fund wrote: "I raged against God, but then I realised it had happened because of man's greed and incompetence"."[33]

John Stott wrote, "Of course originally, disease and death entered the world through sin. But I am now thinking of contemporary sin. Sometimes suffering is due to the sin of others, as when children suffered from unloving or irresponsible parents, the poor and hungry from economic injustice, refugees from the cruelties of war, and road causalities caused by drunken drivers."[34] Can I add to this list from John Stott: suffering caused by the sin of indiscriminate and wanton violence. Suffering can be the consequence of our own sin. But what about the years of the Troubles?

I read about a young, seventeen-year-old Christian being shot dead in a video shop in Belfast. A nine-year boy in Londonderry, happily playing with others, set off a trip wire in his garden and was killed. There are many other examples of people suffering because of the sinful actions of others during the Troubles. There is suffering as a

---

32 Gumbel N. (1994) "Searching Issues" Eastbourne, Kingsway Communications Ltd.
33 Gumbel N. (1994) "Searching Issues" Eastbourne, Kingsway Communications Ltd.
34 Stott, J. (1989), "The Cross of Christ", Leicester, Inter-Varsity Fellowship.

consequence of earthquakes, famines and hurricanes. This suffering has nothing to do with personal sin. Written across the years of the Troubles we witness suffering because of the sin of others.

Where was God in the Troubles?

The Rev Robert Bradford was a Methodist minister in the Suffolk area of Belfast. It was an interface area and the Rev Bradford was involved closely with negotiating with local community leaders and housing agencies as people were bombed out or received threats of worse if they didn't vacate their properties. In August 1971, approximately 200 Protestants fled the area in one night. The same was happening with Catholic families as they were attacked by the Protestant Tartan gangs. Suffolk had a heavy military presence. Every new army commander in the area was advised, "Get to know the IRA Commander, the UDA Commander and Rev Robert Bradford and if you gain the confidence of these three, you will have a fair idea of what is going on in the area." [35] One Sunday night a Lieutenant, Cliff Burrage, and his squad visited the church and stayed for the Gospel service. A friendship developed between the Lieutenant and Rev Bradford. "After one evening service, Cliff followed Robert (Rev Bradford) into the vestry to tell him of his dramatic conversion earlier that week. He explained how he had moved from a position of self-sufficiency to a realization of his need of God's help. He had stepped off the pavement at Horn Drive and, while patrolling, had committed his life to God, stepping onto the opposite pavement as a new believer- a totally new creation."[36]

I was told the story of a group of Christian women in County Armagh, most of whose husbands worked for the security services.

---

35 Bradford N. (2021), "When Time Is Taken", Belfast, Maurice Wylie Media.
36 Bradford N. (2021), "When Time Is Taken", Belfast, Maurice Wylie Media.

The wives would pray together for their loved-ones' safety, especially when their husbands were out on night patrols. Housework was secondary, everything was secondary. From this prayer group a powerful intercessory ministry was established that reached out to many people.

I was talking recently with an Englishman who served in the army in the early 1970's in the border area of Northern Ireland. His name is John. He was unsaved and didn't have any understanding of what the Troubles were about. Out of the blue, and along with other colleagues in the army unit, he received an anonymous card in the post. On the front the card said, "We want you to know that we care for you and we are praying for you." On the back there were these words, "Because Christ loved us, we love you." John was nineteen years of age and was very surprised to receive the card because of all the surrounding hostility they were encountering at the time. John put it in his locker and, said honestly, "I saw it as a lucky charm", but he came to value this little card. In fear he would have secretly prayed, "Please don't let me die". This card became a treasured possession and drew him toward the LORD God. This was the second time in his young life that he had received a Christian witness. The first was in 1975 when he was serving on a destroyer. John told me how these two Christian interventions in his life were important pieces in him coming to faith in 1984.

The next chapter will explore more about the Christian and suffering. There is a scripture that comes to mind from Matthew 5:43-45 and Jesus is teaching:

> *"You have heard that it was said, 'Love your neighbour and hate your enemy.' But I say to you, love your enemies and pray for those who persecute you, so that you may be sons of your Father who is in heaven; for He causes His sun to rise on the evil and the good, and sends rain on the righteous and the unrighteous."* (NASB)

The Christian and Suffering

*"Blessed be the God and Father of
our Lord Jesus Christ,
the Father of mercies and God of all comfort,
who comforts us in all our affliction
so that we will be able to comfort
those who are in any affliction with the comfort
with which we ourselves are comforted by God."*
2 Corinthians 1:3,4 (NASB)

David Prior in his book, "The Suffering and The Glory" quotes something that Florence Nightingale said and then makes a very relevant comment:

"On Whit Sunday 1851 Florence Nightingale wrote: 'My life is more difficult than almost any other kind. My life is more suffering than almost any other kind. Is it not God?' Even after making due allowances for the mentality which sees God's will only in adversity and unpleasantness (everything pleasant being necessarily under suspicion), we can see the thrust of Florence Nightingale's comment on her personal suffering: 'Is it not God?' She is asserting that suffering is natural and normal to the Christian experience. There is a growing trend to deny that. If you really allow God to work in you, it is often affirmed, you will be strong and successful, healthy and victorious.

Conversely, if you suffer, show weakness or vulnerability, you are not being a proper Christian."[37]

David Prior was writing this in 1985. He identified the trend, back in the 1980's, of dissociating suffering from the Christian faith. I would suggest the trend that David Prior identified is now common across the Church. When did you last hear a message about suffering and how the LORD uses suffering to transform us and grow our faith, deepen our devotion and worship of Him, the LORD God? I seriously wonder what some of today's Christian teachers and leaders would say to Paul and the list of sufferings he experienced in his ministry life. You can read about his experiences in 2 Corinthians 11:22-33. Would they say, "Paul, where was your faith? Paul, where was your 'positive confession'?

In the late 1990's Pat, my wife, and I lived and ministered for a number of years in the Highlands of Scotland. Pat had a friend whose mother died and this is what she said, "In my church, there is much rejoicing, but there is no room to mourn."

The Mystery that is Suffering…

I have a book in my library entitled, "God is not Nice".[38] One of the challenges of the book is not to allow our culture to shape our understanding of the Lord and our response to him. For a number of years, I have read through the Bible in a year. I have used various reading plans and year by year I have discovered a God who has done some tough things in people's lives. Things that have caused suffering to people — things that have raised questions in people's minds about God's love, God's presence and God's power.

---

37 Prior D. (1985), "The Suffering and the Glory", London, Hodder and Stoughton.
38 Lehner U. (2017) "God is not Nice", USA, Ave Maria Press.

In the case of Israel, suffering was experienced as a consequence of their disobedience and idolatry before the LORD. But there are other incidents where the Lord appears to allow or even instigate suffering in people's lives.

In 1 Samuel 1:1-7 we have the story of Elkanah, Peninnah and Hannah. It specifically says in reference to Hannah, *"... the LORD had closed her womb."* Peninnah *"had children, but Hannah had no children"*, we are told. Understanding how important the blessing of children was in those days, it is quite a hard thing that the Lord had done. He had closed Hannah's womb for no reason that she could understand at the time.

Hannah went through serious grief from Peninnah, Elkanah's other wife. We read, *"Her rival (Peninnah), however, would provoke her bitterly to irritate her, because the LORD had closed her womb. It happened year after year... she would provoke her; so she wept and would not eat."*

For a number of years Pat and I had the privilege of ministering in Zimbabwe. On one of our visits, we met a Christian couple, who had one child. The family had a huge farm. They had a market garden area the size of four football pitches and that was only one part of this farming enterprise. The farm came under repeated attacks from the army of Robert Mugabe. Over a period of time, day and night, the family experienced intimidation, threats and attack. Mugabe's soldiers were camped around the perimeter of the farm house with drums beating, high on drugs and drink. The family eventually lost their farm and had to flee for their lives. I can still remember the feelings of sadness and wonder, feelings of grief and amazement as I listened to their story. Their son was still suffering from the trauma of the whole incident. Towards the end of telling the story the mother said, "We went to church and professed faith but had begun to take our privileged lifestyle and faith for granted. I am so glad we went through that experience or I would have never come to know God in the way I know Him now. We had become very comfortable in our Christianity. We were self-sufficient on the farm. We had everything we needed." I felt humbled and honoured to be in the presence of such an honest and courageous woman.

There was another interesting aspect to the story. During the standoff with Mugabe's men, the family prayed that the LORD would give them enough time to strip the farm of their personal belongings and business resources before the soldiers took over. And that is what happened. The soldiers just disappeared for no reason and the family were able to ferry away their belongings and farm machinery to a secure warehouse away from the farm. When this was completed, the soldiers suddenly reappeared and eventually they took over the farm.

I can think of another Christian who lived, with his family, in New Zealand. He flew to the UK for a last visit with his father, who was dying of cancer. When he landed in London after a long flight, he received the sad news that his young daughter had been killed in a road accident. He continued his journey to visit his father but then went back to bury his daughter.

There are many reasons for suffering in our lives. There is suffering caused by the sin of others. We can suffer for doing the right thing. We can also suffer as a result of our own sin. We can suffer because of our faith. But then there is suffering which just seems totally out of order and which comes along for no apparent reason or purpose.

Nicky Gumbel writes, "In 1947, a young New Yorker named Glenn Chambers had a lifelong dream to work for God in Ecuador. At the airport on the day of departure, he wanted to send a note to his mother but he didn't have time to buy a card. He noticed a piece of paper on the terminal floor and picked it up. It turned out to be an advertisement with '*Why?*' spread across it. He scribbled his note around the word 'Why?' and put it in the post box.

That night his aeroplane exploded as it hit the 14,000-foot Colombian peak, El Tablazo. When his mother received the note after the news of his death the question burned up at her from the page... '*Why?*' Why does God allow such suffering? This question is the single greatest challenge to the Christian faith. The amount of suffering and its distribution seem to be random and unfair. It outrages and bewilders us.

Theologians and philosophers have wrestled for centuries with the mystery of undeserved suffering, and no one has ever come up with a simple and complete solution. Today and tomorrow's passages are only part of the answer, but each of them gives us some insight. We see that although suffering is never good in itself, God is able to use it for good in a number of ways. God loves you. Your suffering is also God's suffering. He suffers alongside you. Yet he does not always simply remove suffering from your life; he sometimes uses the bad things that happen to bring about his good purposes."[39]

Story of a Christian from the Troubles...

I was given this story by a friend whose uncle suffered badly in the Troubles.

My friend's uncle worked for the Security Forces, and, in 1977, was shot in the head by terrorists and critically wounded. This is something of his story:

---

[39] Gumbel N. Day 25 "God Intended it for Good" Bible in One Year.

"A doctor showed my brother an x-ray of my head as I was being transferred to another hospital. He said, 'Do you see his head? There's not a chance for him.' At the hospital I was operated on, and after about four days I came round, and discovered that I was paralysed on the left side.

About three weeks later, I just all of a sudden threw my legs out of the bed, and I got up and walked. You know, some of the old 'fellas' in that ward nearly had to be put on the heart machine!

They knew I couldn't walk, and I knew I couldn't walk, but I got up and walked. And you know, the Lord, when He does anything, He doesn't do it by half!

Five weeks after the shooting, I had to go through another serious operation. I had to get one of these titanium plates in my head. A day before I went through this operation, I got a card and there was 2 Corinthians 4:8-9 written on the card.

(v8) "We are troubled on every side, yet not distressed; we are perplexed, but not in despair;" verse 9 was underlined;

"Persecuted, but not forsaken; cast down but not destroyed."

And I thought that was a great word to go with into an operation.

I went through that operation the next day and I now have one of these Titanium plates in my head. And you know, my son says I'm bionic now! But I can tell you I'm far from it! But I thank God for the way that I am.

Six weeks after the shooting I was released from the hospital.

God has blessed me in many ways since that incident and I feel I have been drawn much closer to the Saviour.

And you know, like Job of old, Job had his troubles, and at the end of all his testings by satan he could say, 'I **know** that my Redeemer liveth'. And I can say today with more assurance than I could before the shooting, that 'I **know** that my Redeemer liveth'."

This story sets the scene for the chapters that follow: there have been many individuals who suffered bad things during those years of turmoil and violence in Northern Ireland. But these individuals had a faith or found faith, even amidst the heartaches, pain and questions of those years, and it has been their faith which has helped them to move on and find purpose for their lives.

The Bible and suffering…

The Bible has a very rich and deep vein regarding suffering for a Christian – let me give you a sample:

"And after you have suffered a little while, the God of all grace, who has called you to his eternal glory in Christ, will himself restore, confirm, strengthen, and establish you." 1 Peter 5:10 (ESV)

"For I consider that the sufferings of this present time are not worth comparing with the glory that is to be revealed to us." Romans 8:18 (ESV)

"More than that, we rejoice in our sufferings, knowing that suffering produces endurance, and endurance produces character, and character produces hope, and hope does not put us to shame, because God's love has been poured into our hearts through the Holy Spirit who has been given to us." Romans 5:3-5 (ESV)

"Seeing the crowds, he went up on the mountain, and when he sat down, his disciples came to him. And he opened his mouth and taught them, saying: "Blessed are the poor in spirit, for theirs is the kingdom of heaven. "Blessed are those who mourn, for they shall be comforted. "Blessed are the meek, for they shall inherit the earth ..." Matthew 5:1-48 (ESV)

"And we know that for those who love God all things work together for good, for those who are called according to his purpose." Romans 8:28 (ESV)

"Count it all joy, my brothers, when you meet trials of various kinds, for you know that the testing of your faith produces steadfastness. And let steadfastness have its full effect, that you may be perfect and complete, lacking in nothing." James 1:2-4 (ESV)

"I have said these things to you, that in me you may have peace. In the world you will have tribulation. But take heart; I have overcome the world." John 16:33 (ESV)

"Many are the afflictions of the righteous, but the LORD *delivers him out of them all."* Psalm 34:19 (ESV)

"He will wipe away every tear from their eyes, and death shall be no more, neither shall there be mourning, nor crying, nor pain anymore, for the former things have passed away." Revelation 21:4 (ESV)

"For this light momentary affliction is preparing for us an eternal weight of glory beyond all comparison." 2 Corinthians 4:17 (ESV)

"That I may know him and the power of his resurrection, and may share his sufferings, becoming like him in his death." Philippians 3:10 (ESV)

"He was despised and rejected by men; a man of sorrows, and acquainted with grief; and as one from whom men hide their faces he was despised, and we esteemed him not." Isaiah 53:3 (ESV)

"Blessed be the God and Father of our Lord Jesus Christ, the Father of mercies and God of all comfort, who comforts us in all our affliction, so that we may be able to comfort those who are in any affliction, with the comfort with which we ourselves are comforted by God." 2 Corinthians 1:3-4 (ESV)

"Since therefore Christ suffered in the flesh, arm yourselves with the same way of thinking, for whoever has suffered in the flesh has ceased from sin." 1 Peter 4:1 (ESV)

"Who shall separate us from the love of Christ? Shall tribulation, or distress, or persecution, or famine, or nakedness, or danger, or sword?" Romans 8:35 (ESV)

"Bear one another's burdens, and so fulfil the law of Christ." Galatians 6:2 (ESV)

"For as we share abundantly in Christ's sufferings, so through Christ we share abundantly in comfort too." 2 Corinthians 1:5 (ESV)

"When you pass through the waters, I will be with you; and through the rivers, they shall not overwhelm you; when you walk through fire you shall not be burned, and the flame shall not consume you." Isaiah 43:2 (ESV)

"Then Job arose and tore his robe and shaved his head and fell on the ground and worshiped. And he said, 'Naked I came from my mother's womb, and naked shall I return. The LORD gave, and the LORD has taken away; blessed be the name of the LORD.'" Job 1:20-21 (ESV)

"It is good for me that I was afflicted, that I might learn your statutes." Psalm 119:71 (ESV)

"Before I was afflicted, I went astray, but now I keep your word." Psalm 119:67 (ESV)

"This is my comfort in my affliction, that your promise gives me life." Psalm 119:50 (ESV)

"For this is a gracious thing, when, mindful of God, one endures sorrows while suffering unjustly." 1 Peter 2:19 (ESV)

"Casting all your anxieties on him, because he cares for you." 1 Peter 5:7 (ESV)

"For we do not have a high priest who is unable to sympathize with our weaknesses, but one who in every respect has been tempted as we are, yet without sin. Let us then with confidence draw near to the throne of grace, that we may receive mercy and find grace to help in time of need." Hebrews 4:15-16 (ESV)

"But he said to me, "My grace is sufficient for you, for my power is made perfect in weakness." Therefore, I will boast all the more gladly of my weaknesses, so that the power of Christ may rest upon me. For the sake of Christ, then, I am content with weaknesses, insults, hardships, persecutions, and calamities. For when I am weak, then I am strong." 2 Corinthians 12:9-10 (ESV)

There is a real treasure of truth in these scriptures and throughout the Bible regarding suffering in our Christian lives. Every angle is covered – personal hope, community support, spiritual understanding and, best of all, the presence of the LORD is guaranteed.

The Sufferings of Jesus…

"In 1967, a beautiful athletic teenager named Joni Eareckson had a terrible diving accident at Chesapeake Bay, which left her a quadriplegic. Gradually, after bitterness, anger, rebellion and despair, she came to trust the sovereignty of God. She built a new life of painting (using her mouth to hold the paintbrush), singing and public speaking. One night, three years after the accident, she realised that Jesus empathized with her completely. It had not occurred to her before that, on the cross, Jesus was in a similar pain to hers, unable to move, also paralysed."[40]

The writer to the Hebrews tells us that we have a Saviour who is able *"to sympathize"* with us in our pains, our hurts and wounds.

> *"Though now ascended up on high,*
> *He bends on earth a brother's eye;*
> *Partaker of the human name,*
> *He knows the frailty of our frame.*
> *Our fellow-suff'rer yet retains*
> *A fellow-feeling of our pains;*
> *And still remembers in the skies*
> *His tears, his agonies, and cries.*
> *In ev'ry pang that rends the heart,*
> *The Man of sorrows had a part;*
> *He sympathizes with our grief,*
> *And to the suff'rer sends relief."*
> Scottish Psalter[41] (Hebrews 4:15)

Jesus suffered flogging, beatings, mockery, injustice, rejection, excruciating pain from nails in his feet and hands, heat stroke, thirst, unnatural body posture, difficulty in breathing, abandonment, spitting, blood seeping from his body and head, hunger, nakedness, betrayal, the suffering of family and friends and, beyond all that the unimaginable anguish of bearing the sins of the whole world and being separated from His Father.

---

40 Gumbel N. (1994) "Searching Issues" Eastbourne, Kingsway Communications Ltd

41 Preceptaustin.org

A number of years ago a film came out called, "The Passion of the Christ." I never watched it personally but I heard, from those who viewed the film, the scene at the Cross was very graphic and gory. It caused people to weep and feel something, of what Jesus suffered for us. Jesus spent six hours on the Cross in constant pain, physically, emotionally and spiritually.

The Message[42] paraphrase says –

> *"He was beaten, he was tortured,*
> *but he didn't say a word.*
> *Like a lamb taken to be slaughtered*
> *and like a sheep being sheared,*
> *he took it all in silence.*
> *Justice miscarried, and he was led off—*
> *and did anyone really know what was happening?*
> *He died without a thought for his own welfare,*
> *beaten bloody for the sins of my people."* Isaiah 53:7-8.

We have a Saviour who has plumbed the depths of pain and sorrow as a consequence of the sins of others. He knows the thoughts that come into our minds when we are heartbroken over a death. He knows the questions that we will ask when pain comes into our lives. He knows the temptations that will arise when we suffer unjustly: temptations to seek revenge and retribution. He knows the thoughts, but He also knows the feelings that arise when we suffer at the hands of others.

He is able to enter into our griefs; He is able to share in our pains, He is able to mourn with us because HE has been there HIMSELF.

This knowledge, the heart empathy, the ability to enter into our pains comes from his own experience at the hands of "wicked men". Joni

---

42 The Message: The Bible in Contemporary Language 2004 Eugene H. Peterson.

realised that Jesus empathized with her because of the hours he spent on the Cross paralysed. The same is true for us when we wrestle with the hurts, wounds and scars inflicted by the sinful actions of others.

A story: What is Possible?

This headline appeared in The Christian Post on June 8, 2011:

> **Christian Mother Shows Faith to Forgive and Love Son's Killer.**

The story, written by Daniel Blake, a contributor to The Christian Post, is as follows:

> "A devout Christian mother whose son was brutally shot dead has shown amazing forgiveness by reconciling with his killer and even inviting the man to move in as her neighbour. The killing happened in February 1993, when Mary Johnson's son, Laramiun Byrd, 20, was shot dead by 16-year-old Oshea Israel after a dispute at a party in Minneapolis, Minnesota.
>
> Israel, who at the time was caught up in drugs and gangs, served 17 years in prison for the killing. However, he has now moved in next door to Johnson, 59, in what can only be described as an incredible act of kindness and forgiveness.
>
> Johnson confessed that in the immediate aftermath of her son's killing she wanted Israel imprisoned. According to The Daily Mail she said, 'My son was gone. I was angry and hated this boy, hated his mother.' She explained how her son's death had hit her 'like a tsunami'. She said, 'I wanted him to be caged up like the animal he was.'

Johnson went on to establish an organization that supports people in a similar situation; mothers whose children had been killed. Over time Johnson felt a greater and greater urge to meet Israel face-to-face and explore whether she could really practice forgiveness as her faith in Jesus had taught her. Israel was shocked by the request and refused to meet his victim's mother at first. However, nine months later he himself had a change of heart and agreed to meet. Israel described their first meeting: 'I believe the first thing she said to me was, 'Look, you don't know me. I don't know you. Let's just start with right now.' And I was befuddled myself.'

The meetings continued on a regular basis after that, and upon Israel's release from prison 18 months ago, Johnson has helped Israel's reintegration into society. She even amazingly introduced Israel, now 34, to her landlord and gave her blessing for him to move in next door to her. Johnson has explained that the close friendship she now shares with Israel has only been due to her deep Christian beliefs. She said, 'Unforgiveness is like cancer. It will eat you from the inside out. It's not about that other person, me forgiving him does not diminish what he's done. Yes, he murdered my son – but the forgiveness is for me.' According to the Daily Mail, Israel commented: 'I haven't totally forgiven myself yet, I'm learning to forgive myself. And I'm still growing toward trying to forgive myself.' He now insists he wants to prove himself to Johnson, and wants to contribute to society. He now visits prisons and churches, often with Johnson by his side, to tell their story and talk on the topics of forgiveness and reconciliation."

The stories...

In chapters 3 -7, I tell five stories of people who suffered at the hands of terrorists.

"These murders, of four fathers and one brother-in-law, took place between the years 1983-1985. In these three years 217 people died in the Troubles."[43]

By way of context, some of the key incidents of these years were[44] -

- A judge and the daughter of a magistrate were murdered by the IRA. Both were killed as they left a Catholic Church.

- 36 people were jailed on the evidence of UVF and IRA supergrasses. In the case of the evidence supplied by an IRA super-grass, 22 were jailed, in total, for more than 4,000 years. But the use of super-grass evidence backfired at the end of 1984. Fourteen loyalist prisoners, jailed on the evidence of a UVF super-grass were released. The evidence given by a republican super-grass was not accepted and thirty-five defendants were released.

- This period saw the start of political initiatives and discussions to resolve the Northern Ireland situation e.g.: the New Ireland Forum; the Anglo-Irish Intergovernmental Council and the Anglo-Irish Agreement. This latter document resulted in an estimated 100,000 Unionists gathering in Belfast to voice their opposition. The first meeting of the Anglo-Irish Intergovernmental Conference resulted in all fifteen Unionist MPs resigning to force by-elections.

---

43 McKittrick D., Feeney B., Thornton C. and Kelters S. (1999) "Lost Lives. The stories of the men, women and children who died as a result of the Northern Ireland Troubles", Edinburgh, Mainstream Publishing Company Ltd.

44 McKittrick D. & McVea D. (2012) "Making Sense of the Troubles", London, Viking (an imprint of Penguin Books).

- Gerry Adams was elected as a Westminster MP; he was also elected as president of Sinn Fein(SF)[45]; an attempt was made on his life by the UDA and the United States refused him a visa for a visit. In local government elections SF won a number of council seats. This resulted in Unionists disrupting some meetings.

- Portadown became a flashpoint because of the re-routing of Orange Order[46] parades. There was rioting and more than 500 police homes across Northern Ireland were attacked; 150 officers were forced to move homes. In Portadown a loyalist was killed by a plastic bullet; the first and only Protestant plastic bullet death.

- There was the kidnapping of a supermarket executive and two were killed in the rescue; one was an Irish soldier and the other a Garda[47] cadet.

- There were bomb attacks on Harrods in London and at the Conservative party conference hotel in Brighton.

- Seven tons of arms and ammunition intended for the IRA were recovered from a boat off the Irish coast. This was the biggest arms seizure since the 1973 capture of the Claudia.

- Peter Robinson, with a group of loyalists, staged a late-night invasion into County Monaghan (a county in the Republic of Ireland) to highlight the inadequate border security. He was arrested, pleaded guilty in the southern court and paid a £15,000 fine for unlawful assembly.

---

45 Sinn Féin is an Irish republican and democratic socialist political party active throughout both the Republic of Ireland and Northern Ireland. During the Troubles, Sinn Féin was associated with the Provisional Irish Republican Army (IRA). (Wikipedia).

46 The Loyal Orange Institution, commonly known as the Orange Order, is an international Protestant fraternal order based in Northern Ireland and primarily associated with Ulster Protestants, particularly those of Ulster Scots heritage. (Wikipedia).

47 Garda – Ireland's National Police and Security Service.

These were some of the incidents during the years 1983-1985. Sinn Fein were rising as a political force within Northern Ireland. The Republicans were still arming themselves, although political discussions had started to resolve the situation. Tit-for-tat killings were still the order of the day. Unionist politicians were on high alert to ensure that their views were taken into account at any governmental discussions between Dublin and London. The Unionist community were endeavouring to protect their traditions and culture. But the civilian population was still suffering. Five were killed and eighty were injured in the Harrods bombing. Two Catholics were killed as they were leaving a place of worship.

The Story of Rodney Wilson

"The Lord is good, a strong refuge when trouble comes. He is close to those who trust in him." Nahum 1:7 (NLT)

On Sunday 20th November 1983 the Irish National Liberation Army (INLA)[48] attacked Mountain Lodge Pentecostal Church in Darkley, South Armagh. People from the local community and further afield had come together for the Sunday evening service, which started at 6pm. There were approximately seventy people in the wooden building; fifty adults and twenty children. Several songs had already been sung when the pastor of the church, Bob Bain, came forward to lead the congregation in the opening hymn, "Have you been to Jesus for the cleansing power?"

David Bell, the present pastor of the church, who was in the service that night, wrote, "The congregation had just begun to sing the final verse, 'Lay aside the garments that are stained by sin.' And then it happened. For a moment, we all thought someone was throwing pebbles against the outside of the window panes, on that wintry November evening. It sounded just like the rattle of small stones on a tin roof. After all, very few of us had ever heard the sound of gun fire before! It took a few minutes for the reality of what was happening to sink in. Falling to the floor for cover, we realised all too quickly what

---

48 The Irish National Liberation Army (INLA) is an Irish republican socialist paramilitary group formed on 10 December 1974, during the 30-year period of conflict known as «the Troubles". It is the paramilitary wing of the Irish Republican Socialist Party.

was taking place – somehow our church had become the latest target in the Northern Ireland 'Troubles'."[49]

Three church elders were murdered in this attack: Harold Brown aged 59, Victor Cunningham aged 39 and David Wilson aged 44. As a consequence, three women were widowed and seven children lost their fathers.

According to the Irish Times:[50] "Harold Brown, Victor Cunningham and David Wilson were standing at the church's front porch discussing a friend who was in hospital. Their job was to welcome people to the gospel service and find them a seat. Harold and Victor were gunned down immediately and died where they fell, whilst David staggered wounded through the doors into the main meeting room in an attempt to raise the alarm and shout for people to get down. He stumbled the full length of the aisle and died in a small room behind the platform.

At least three gunmen then stood outside the hall and strafed it, wounding seven more people as bullets passed through the thin wooden walls.[51] Up to 40 shots were fired into the church. One of the injured sustained five bullet wounds to the stomach; one woman was hit in the spine and another had her elbow smashed by a bullet. This small wooden church, was situated on a hill, in a mainly Catholic village, not far from the border."

---

49 Bell D. (2013) "Fire on the Mountain", Belfast, Ambassador Books and Media.
50 The Irish Times is a daily newspaper, based in Dublin. I have corrected a few mistakes in this account. Quotes taken from – McKittrick D., Feeney B., Thornton C. and Kelters S. (1999) "Lost Lives. The stories of the men, women and children who died as a result of the Northern Ireland Troubles", Edinburgh, Mainstream Publishing Company Ltd.
51 Bell D (see 50 above) tells us: "Miraculously, the automatic machine gun the terrorists were using jammed. This most certainly saved additional lives, although by now a number of people were dead and several others had suffered serious injuries."

As the Irish Times described it: "The Monaghan border curves less than two miles away. With all its lights blazing, the little hall stood out on a hill, the easiest of targets."

"The pastor's son said everything had been normal until he heard two or three single bangs during the last verse of a hymn. Then there were three or four more bangs. 'The door flew open and Davy Wilson who had been standing in the front hall came running in', he said. 'I was still standing at this stage and could see blood coming from Davy's mouth and nose. He was trying to talk but I couldn't hear what he was saying'.

More shots were fired as David Wilson ran and there was a burst of gunfire directed at the front hall. Pastor Bob Bain, who was conducting the service said, 'It came just like a flash of lightening through the window to us. We didn't understand what was happening until it was half through. Somebody said, 'Get down,' and everybody dived. The people reacted marvelously. The doctor said he had never seen a place for such an atrocity to happen that the people were so calm. Nobody was screaming. There were children under their seats at the front, and except for them nobody cried."[52] This tragedy was described as "an act of sectarian slaughter on a worshipping community which goes beyond any previous deed of violence."[53]

Pastor David Bell in his book, "Fire on the Mountain"[54] tells us more about the injured. The person who sustained five bullets in the stomach was William Whyte. "He was bleeding profusely when Pastor Bob (Bain) came down to the back of the hall to pray for him. As he

---

52 McKittrick D., Feeney B., Thornton C. and Kelters S. (1999) "Lost Lives. The stories of the men, women and children who died as a result of the Northern Ireland Troubles", Edinburgh, Mainstream Publishing Company Ltd.
53 McKittrick D., Feeney B., Thornton C. and Kelters S. (1999) "Lost Lives. The stories of the men, women and children who died as a result of the Northern Ireland Troubles", Edinburgh, Mainstream Publishing Company Ltd.
54 Bell D. (2013) "Fire on the Mountain", Belfast, Ambassador Books and Media.

prayed the prayer of faith, the bleeding ceased immediately. However, the local doctor was of the opinion that so extensive were his wounds that it was unlikely that William would still be alive by the time he reached the hospital." William did survive. "William's wife's spine was grazed by another bullet; just millimeters separated her from being paralysed. Miraculously, a bullet passed through the trouser leg of their young son of just 18 months, without even grazing his flesh."

The woman whose elbow was injured was Pastor Bain's daughter, Sally. David Bell would go on to marry Sally, and together they have led the church at Mountain Lodge for over 25 years. A bullet "passed through her (Sally's) elbow joint, totally demolishing it, and lodged in her thigh." The doctors, at the local hospital, discussed amputating Sally's right arm at the elbow. The decision was deferred and an alternative solution was put in place; Sally was fitted with a brace that was strapped around her upper and lower arm. The doctors informed Sally "that this was going to be her lot for life." Sally had a promise from the LORD: "I am the Lord that healeth thee." Through prayer and by faith, a day came when Sally was able to raise her arm without the aid of a brace. This was something that the doctors said would never happen. "Finally, they (doctors) discharged her, concluding that a 'Greater Power' obviously had been at work."

There were others injured in this attack. One man suffered physical pain from his bullet wound for the rest of his life. Another still bears the scar of a bullet that grazed her cheek and, finally, another required bone restructuring and plastic surgery.

The Wilson family...

David (Davy) Wilson was the father of Rodney and Esther Wilson. The Wilson family were a farming family; David, Doreen (wife), Rodney (son), and Esther (daughter) all worked the farm together.

In May 2011, The Restoring Hope Project Team, Crossfire Trust[55], produced a book called "We All Get On Well But ...". In this publication Rodney wrote about his life before the tragedy of his father's murder.

"My name is Rodney Wilson. I grew up on the family farm with Dad, Mum, my sister Esther and Auntie Yvonne just 2 miles from Keady. Now I live there with my wife Hilary and our 3 children, Leah, David and Joshua.

My childhood days are filled with happy memories of school life and helping Dad on the farm. I would go with him at any opportunity to the livestock markets in Keady and Newtownhamilton to buy cattle and pigs and often we enjoyed a cup of tea with the many farmers he knew there. The summer holidays were always busy making hay and silage etc., but we always managed to get a family holiday to Portstewart for a few days in August before the new school year began.

The troubles were rife as I grew up and as my Granddad and Granny's farm was on the border. I still remember the sights and sounds of the big green Saracens, the chopping of the helicopters overhead, the regular army checkpoints and the many news reports of shootings and bombings, which unfortunately in those days became the 'norm.'

In the late 1970's, Dad looked seriously at selling up and moving to Scotland to farm, just as many of his friends and relatives had done. This never materialized and now I often wonder how different life would have been if we had relocated at that time.

---

55 Crossfire Trust are a charitable organisation operating on a cross community and cross border basis within South Armagh. They run a wide range of community support and good relations projects, provide supported accommodation and bring communities together to nurture cohesiveness across all divides.

I was blessed to have been brought up in a Christian home and as a young boy I came to a personal faith in Jesus Christ for myself." Rodney was 7 years old when he became a Christian.

Rodney had a fear of dying without knowing the Lord Jesus as his Saviour and so he 'asked Jesus into' his heart and life. 'From that moment the fear of dying without knowing that I would be in Heaven was gone, and I knew peace with God and the hope of eternal life with Christ. Ten years later that hope was to be the anchor in the severe and unexpected storm of loss and separation.'"[56]

The Grief of a Daughter...

Esther wrote: "My dad was not involved with the security forces, and therefore we didn't need to take extra measures to ensure safety, as so many others did at that time. We didn't need to look under the car for booby traps before we set out on a journey, or keep looking behind our backs to make sure we were not being targeted. Safety was not an issue for us.

As a family, we attended a small church at Mountain Lodge, where my dad was an elder. My parents had brought us up to respect both Catholics and Protestants in our border town community, and at a young age I followed their example in developing a simple faith in Jesus. It was a faith that was to be severely tested during a church service, the year I turned twelve."[57]

Chapter 1 mentions something of the healing process that Esther has gone through as a consequence of her father's murder. It was 15 years

---

56 Bell D. (2013) "Fire on the Mountain", Belfast, Ambassador Books and Media.
57 Bell D. (2013) "Fire on the Mountain", Belfast, Ambassador Books and Media.

after his death that Esther commenced her journey of healing. Esther was 27 years old.

"At this time, I began to envisage my dad's death from a different perspective, seeing it as the same process that births an oak tree. A small acorn, planted in the ground, has to be broken and die in order for new life to emerge. In the dark, its roots are being formed and are making their way deep into the soil – roots that will be needed to make the resulting tree stand tall and strong.

Armed with this new perspective, I found a framed picture in a drawer of our home, with the inscription which read, 'A tree has been planted in Israel in memory of David Wilson, who died November 20, 1983.' I went back to re-read newspapers from the time of the event, as well as the large number of sympathy cards we'd received. There was a letter with my name on it. It was a letter from a friend of my dad's that I did not recall having ever received. In the letter, that friend told me what my dad had been like and why I should be proud to be his daughter. The process of healing continued and took root in my heart.

When Jesus hung on the cross, He said, 'Father, forgive them, for they know not what they do.' (Luke 23:34). Through his pain He still had time for the thief hanging beside Him. Even on the cross, He still heard the cry of the broken. Darkness covered the earth that day, just as darkness hung over the earth the night of November 20, 1983, when my dad laid down his life to save us.

Whatever those gunmen had come to accomplish, their plans had been thwarted. I learned to sing, 'You give and take away, but my heart will choose to say, Lord blessed be Your Name.' Now, as a worship leader, those words are very real to me, and a source of great comfort. God continues to give me many father figures in my life."[58]

Rodney's story...

Rodney and Esther were in the service and sitting with their mother when the attack took place on Sunday 20th November 1983. The evening service started at 6.00pm.

"It was a normal Sunday evening in November. After we had done the usual chores on the farm, Mum, my sister Esther and I set off for the meeting at Mountain Lodge. Dad had already left for the service with David Bell who regularly came to our home on Sunday afternoon's.

We had a habit of being late and this particular Sunday was no exception. It was about ten past six when we walked into the porch and those present were already singing the opening hymn, 'Have you been to Jesus for the cleansing power, are you washed in the blood of the Lamb?'

We were welcomed by Dad, Harold and Victor. Dad remained in the porch chatting with them, as the rest of us made our way in. We found a seat and joined in the singing.

Suddenly I was startled by a strange loud noise, the doors behind us burst open, and the next thing I saw was Dad running up the aisle shouting 'Get down, get down!' He ran to the front of the hall and out through a door at the side of the pulpit into the kitchen. I then realised we were being attacked by gunmen. The gunfire continued for what seemed like an eternity.

---

[58] Bell D. (2013) "Fire on the Mountain", Belfast, Ambassador Books and Media.

When all the noise had stopped there was an eerie silence before everyone started to get up and move around in a daze. I went to look for Dad. I found him on the kitchen floor where he lay motionless. I couldn't believe that he had been shot. Someone confirmed my worst fears and told me he was dead. I thought that as I had just seen him run up the hall, he was ok. Sadly, this was not the case and I couldn't believe what had just happened. Was it for real?

I soon realised that Dad was not the only person shot dead that evening, but Harold and Victor had been killed too. The whole scene was unbelievable and unimaginable and it was hard for me to comprehend that it was really happening.

The terrorists were not expecting to encounter anyone on the porch. I believe their intentions were to open fire on a whole congregation from the rear. It was the presence of Dad, Harold and Victor that startled them and saved many lives including my own. They opened fire on the three men and even though Dad had been shot and wounded, he found strength to run up the hall to warn us and also ensure the front outside door was closed to prevent them from entering the hall from that direction and possibly causing more deaths."[59]

In the service that evening there was a family from Enniskillen. The Kenny family (Ronnie, Edith, and three children: Stephen, Ronnie Junior and Janet) had been invited to come and sing and preach the Gospel. Edith was grazed by a bullet: "I felt a stinging sensation on the right side of my face". Janet discovered that there was a bullet hole in the hymn book she had been singing from. Edith says, "We moved forward after the shooting stopped and found David Wilson had died. His wife and two children were by his side, his young son saying to my husband, 'That's my daddy'."[60]

---

59 Bell D. (2013) "Fire on the Mountain", Belfast, Ambassador Books and Media.
60 Bell D. (2013) "Fire on the Mountain", Belfast, Ambassador Books and Media.

The Aftermath and the Funeral…

There was widespread condemnation of the hideous shooting at Mountain Lodge. Dr John Armstrong, Church of Ireland Primate said, "This truly horrifying slaughter is a terrifying example of hate. Those who in any way support the perpetrators of these and other murders are no less guilty than the killers themselves."[61]

Dr John Armstrong also said, "This tragedy to me is an assault on a most sacred freedom – the freedom to worship. It must be the worst incident ever in Northern Ireland's 14 years of troubles."[62]

Rodney related how the community was affected by these murders: "The whole community was horrified and numbed by what had taken place. Many from a Roman Catholic upbringing were greatly embarrassed and felt let down by those who claimed to represent that section of the community. They said, 'It should not have happened'." The group who claimed responsibility for the atrocity called themselves the Catholic Reaction Force.[63]

There was genuine upset, especially because a place of worship was involved. Cardinal Tomas O'Fiaich[64] said, "The slaughter of three innocent people and the serious wounding of several others is an unspeakable crime. But to carry out this deed when they were at prayer in their local place of worship adds the guilt of sacrilege and blasphemy to that murder. It is a direct attack on the God whom

---

[61] Armagh Observer Thursday 24th November 1983.

[62] Armagh Observer Thursday 24th November 1983.

[63] The attackers were rogue members of the Irish National Liberation Army (INLA). They claimed responsibility using the cover name «Catholic Reaction Force», saying it was retaliation for recent sectarian attacks on Catholics by the loyalist «Protestant Action Force». The attack was condemned by INLA leadership. A week after the attack, the INLA admitted that one of the gunmen had been an INLA member and admitted supplying him with the gun, (Wikipedia).

[64] Cardinal Tomas O'Fiaich was the Primate of All Ireland. Armagh Observer Thursday 24th November 1983.

they were worshipping. To those who perpetrated this atrocity I say, 'Don't care to claim the name of Catholic' for your band of evil doers. The Catholics of this area abhor your crime and never want to hear of you again."

This horrific attack touched the world. Rodney said, "It was international news because of where it happened. Not because of the numbers but because the target was a wooden hut and a place of worship. The congregation were no threat to anyone. There was no one in the security forces present on that evening as far as I am aware."

David Bell, in his book called "Fire on the Mountain" highlights the comments that were made in the British Parliament and includes examples of letters and telegrams that Pastor Bain received from around the world expressing their sadness and shock at this tragedy.

Victor's funeral service took place on Tuesday 22nd November, while Harold and David's were on Wednesday 23rd. There were well over one thousand mourners at each funeral.

"A mile long queue of cars wound its way through Keady and around the border countryside to the home of father of two Mr. David Wilson (44) from Killreavy. There was a service in the two-storey farm house on top of the hill overlooking the church half a mile away, where interment followed."[65] Rodney remembers that the funeral "was massive" and mentioned how "even today people say to me, 'I was at your dad's funeral'."

Politicians, local councillors, local priests, nuns and Protestants from all denominations joined the mourners at the funeral. The minister, Rev. Lynch, who gave a strong Gospel challenge in the church and

---

65 Ulster Gazette 1st December 1983 (see Bell D. (2013) "Fire on the Mountain", Belfast, Ambassador Books and Media.)

around the grave, highlighted David Wilson's testimony of faith and that he knew that God had prepared a place for him in Heaven. The article in the Ulster Gazette included this paragraph: "The service ended and the coffin was borne out of the church to the graveside. It was now almost dark. The family circle joined in the singing of the hymn 'There's a land that is fairer than day'."[66]

The Historical Enquiry Team[67] did review the murders at Mountain Lodge Pentecostal Church. The comment was made that the attack was for publicity. Rodney was interviewed by the team and was able to ask questions. The conclusion of the enquiry was that the attack was "pure sectarian, there was no other motive. This was a group of Protestants: "an easy target near the border." No one has ever been found guilty of this heinous crime against innocent Christian people.

Rodney's grief...

Following the shooting, Rodney couldn't remember exactly who took the family home. "I don't remember a lot of screaming and crying and I couldn't believe that Dad was dead. We gathered ourselves together and went home. It was hard to believe and we were in a state of numbness." They left before the police and emergency services arrived.

Rodney said, "The next few days were somewhat of a blur as Dad's funeral preparations got under way. Many people came to offer us support and help. Dad's funeral was well attended like the others but apart from that, I can't remember much more about it and I put that down to the immense grief and loss I was feeling at the time. In the

---

66 Ulster Gazette 1st December 1983 (see Bell D. (2013) "Fire on the Mountain", Belfast, Ambassador Books and Media.)

67 The Historical Enquiries Team was a unit of the Police Service of Northern Ireland set up in September 2005 to investigate the 3,269 unsolved murders committed during the Troubles, specifically between 1968 and 1998. It was wound up in September 2014, when the PSNI restructured following budget cuts. (Wikipedia).

days that followed, Dad was sorely missed. We had grown very close as he and I worked on the family farm together."[68]

Rodney remembers his father as a kind and generous person, hard-working and non-sectarian in outlook and attitude, who tried to live at peace with everyone. The farm where David was born was close to the border with the Republic of Ireland and neighbours, both Protestant and Catholic, helped each other and shared machinery as needed.

Rodney's father had come to faith in the Lord Jesus through the Faith Mission[69] holding Gospel meetings in the area. David loved going to Christian meetings and was involved with the Full Gospel Business Men's Fellowship International Craigavon Chapter[70]. Rodney told us how his father was not afraid to pray with people, whatever the need was. The family knew their identity was British but this did not make them bigoted or anti-Catholic in any way.

Mrs Wilson...

Mrs Wilson's mother died when she was 6 years old and her father when she was in her late teens. Because she was the oldest daughter, she inherited the family farm and continued to run it with help from her sister Yvonne who lived with her. When she married David in 1965, he came to live on the farm with them.

---

68 Bell D. (2013) "Fire on the Mountain", Belfast, Ambassador Books and Media.

69 Faith Mission is a Christian mission committed **"to reach through passionate evangelism the lost of all age groups, particularly in the villages and rural areas of Great Britain and Ireland, and by biblical teaching to encourage holiness of heart and life in Christian people."** See faithmission.org

70 Full Gospel Business Men's Fellowship International (FGBMFI) is the largest network of Christian Businessmen in the world. Founded in 1952, they are in over 85 nations – meeting in thousands of chapters. See fgbmfi.org.

Three weeks after the atrocity, Rodney returned to the Armagh Royal School were he completed his A-levels and then went on to Queens University Belfast to complete a degree in agriculture. While at school, Rodney would work on the farm evenings and weekends and when he studied in Belfast he came home every weekend to help his mother, aunt and sister on the farm. To enable Rodney to further his education, the pig enterprise ceased and the cattle herd was halved. As well as this, the grandparents farm was leased out to a neighbouring farmer.

Two friends were a real help with the farm in the early days. Jim Dougan was a bus driver who would come up to the farm after finishing his early morning shift and help with the feeding of the cattle. David Walker, a neighbouring farmer, "was a great source of advice and help as well as a mentor who was always on the end of the phone to assist with a cow calving".

In the book, "We All Get on Well But …", Rodney wrote, "I will always be grateful for the help and support we received from neighbours, friends and relatives which enabled Mum to carry on the farm business while I completed my studies in Queens University, Belfast. We were always conscious of being carried by prayer from the many churches and prayer groups throughout the land and further afield in those dark days."[71]

Rodney pays tribute to his mother's resilience: "I have seen her cry and it was heart-breaking. She lost her husband and has had to grow old on her own. Remember she had already lost a lot with her parents dying while she was so young." Towards the end of the 1990's, the farm was transferred to Rodney and his mother retired to live close to Armagh City.

---

71 "We All Get on Well But …" (May 2011) The Restoring Hope Project Team, Crossfire Trust.

Rodney's Faith…

Rodney came to faith in the Lord Jesus at the age of seven. He had been under conviction for a few months. "There were a lot of sermons about the coming of the Lord and the signs of His coming. I had a fear of being left behind and could not sleep at nights with this fear." After one particular meeting at Mountain Lodge, when Harry Creighton spoke, Rodney says, "I went home and got by my bed and committed my life to Jesus. I told my mum the next morning and the assurance came. It was more about fear than the love of God. After that I had no fear. I had peace."

Rodney wrote in later years, "This decision would be the foundation, comfort and hope that would enable me at the age of 17 to face the days, months and years that would follow the dark night of November 20, 1983, when Dad and his two friends were suddenly and unexpectedly taken into eternity by gunmen while attending a service at Mountain Lodge Pentecostal Church."[72]

A little time after the murder of his father, Rodney had another spiritual experience which helped him move on in his life. He was at a meeting at Corkley Hall. An invitation was given for people to receive the fullness of the Holy Spirit. Rodney said, "I went forward and got filled with the Holy Spirit and spoke in tongues. That was an enablement. An empowerment. That made singing and worship more real."

In the years following the death of his father, Rodney has clearly grown in his faith. He served for many years as a worship leader with his sister Esther, who played the keyboard, and together they would lead people into the presence of God.

---

72 "We All Get on Well But …" (May 2011) The Restoring Hope Project Team, Crossfire Trust.

Regarding his career, Rodney writes, "Since leaving university I have been working with The Ulster Farmers' Union in Armagh. My job has enabled me to meet and do business with lots of people in the area. People who knew Dad often talk about his godly character and how he always had time for everyone. He had many friends from both communities and I am often heartened by many of the stories they share with me while visiting their homes."[73]

He related a story about a wake that he had attended recently. There was a particular Catholic businessman present for whom Rodney has a lot of time, and they would always talk together whenever their paths crossed. This man introduced Rodney to his wife with these words, "This is Rodney whose dad was killed. Rodney is a tremendous example of a Christian who hasn't lived in the past but has forgiven and moved on in his life."

Rodney was very encouraged by the commendation. "It was lovely. It proved that I had moved on. I had done something right and this was coming from a Catholic man."

Rodney still misses his father but he has moved on. Career, marriage, Christian service, having his own family and all the responsibilities that that brings have helped. Understandably, he rejects that well-known saying, 'forgive and forget': "That is totally wrong. It is impossible to forget. You cannot forget what happened. Forgive, 'yes', but forget, 'no'." Rodney is certainly not living in the past and has chosen to move forward with his life.

Rodney's Journey of Forgiveness...

In 2011 Rodney wrote, "There are many 'why's?' that remain unanswered and one that is often asked is – 'Why kill innocent

---

[73] "We All Get on Well But …" (May 2011) The Restoring Hope Project Team, Crossfire Trust.

people in a place of worship?' And although I have many questions left unanswered, I rest in one of the key principles of the Christian life – that is 'forgiveness'. Jesus in the Bible taught us to pray using the Lord's Prayer. It contains the phrase '… forgive us this day our trespasses as we forgive those who trespass against us.' I have found by dealing scripturally with the situations and problems in my life my painful experiences can make me better – not bitter. Today I enjoy the freedom that comes from the power of forgiveness and letting go of the past. Whilst I will never forget Dad who gave his life that dark night, I have decided not to dwell there. A favourite quotation of mine is by Eleanor Roosevelt – 'Yesterday is History, Tomorrow is Mystery, Today is a Gift – that's why we call it the present'."[74]

Rodney's story is very powerful and God honouring. The reason for this is because he chose to handle all the challenges following the killing of his father, God's way. He outlines the following points:

Firstly – the hope of the Gospel. "This has been a big driver. I know that when Dad was murdered, he went to be with the Lord. For me and the family that hope carried us through in the early days. One day we will meet him again. I often think that Dad was young when he was shot. It saved him from growing old. He was blessed. He got to see his Lord earlier than us."

Secondly – a conscious decision: "I chose early on not to blame God. As a consequence, I probably developed a deeper relationship with Him and as a consequence live in the comfort and trust that comes from reading His word. I would take His word and apply it to my life. Knowing the word and not doing it is useless. Scriptures like: 'forgive and you will be forgiven', 'more blessed to give', 'judge not and you will not be judged' are to be lived out. I have a daily Bible reading plan which includes a chapter from both the Old and the New Testaments.

---

[74] "We All Get on Well But …" (May 2011) The Restoring Hope Project Team, Crossfire Trust.

This is gold for life. I keep telling people that the Bible is up to date and relevant. Its wisdom is a life saver. Personally, I don't know how people live without a relationship with the Lord Jesus Christ."

Thirdly – asking questions about his father's death. The main question was not, "Where were you God?" but "Why would you let this happen?" Rodney said, "This was a big question at the time. We knew about the protection of the blood and we were singing "are you washed" at the time. It was a bit of a disappointment: singing about the blood and this happens. God could have stopped it and didn't. We were no threat to anyone."

Rodney has asked some important questions of the Lord about this tragedy but he learned and taught himself what the Bible says regarding tough things happening in life. He has found the disciplines of the Christian life invaluable and it is these that have brought him to a place of contentment and forgiveness in his life. "It didn't happen overnight", he explained. He is not looking for justice in this life, because he has found a better person and a better life to live as a follower of the Lord Jesus Christ.

Fourthly – God has brought fruit out of tragedy. Rodney acknowledges how this family tragedy has affected his character. He wonders what kind of person he would have been if the murder of his father had not taken place. He recognizes a resilience in his character and that his coping mechanisms are strong. He wonders if he would have had the same commitment to prayer and Bible reading if this had not happened. He sees that through the pain of his own heart he has been able to empathise with and minister to others who have suffered in a similar way to himself.

Scripture Verse...

The verse of scripture that Rodney chose to headline his story is from Nahum 1:7: *"The Lord is good, a strong refuge when trouble comes. He is close to those who trust in him."*

At one point, while I was working on this story, there was a song playing in the background. The song, written by David Ruis, was being sung by Robin Mark. The words of the chorus were –

> "We will break dividing walls
> We will break dividing walls
> We will break dividing walls in the name of Your Son
> We will break dividing walls
> We will break dividing walls
> We will break dividing walls
> We will break dividing walls and we will be one."

Rodney could have allowed "dividing walls" to exist in his life as a result of the murder of his father. He was 17 years of age and had his life ahead of him. He could have chosen the revenge route and just increased the cycle of violence that was all around him in South Armagh. But, through faith and obedience to God's Word he never let dividing walls be erected in his life. There is no doubt that the pain and the heartache of losing his father and seeing the suffering of his mother and younger sister were unbearable at times. There must have been many dark days and nights.

Rodney shines as an example of how faith in the Lord Jesus, obedience to His word and a heart that choses to trust in the Lord, mean that our bad experiences don't have to result in a future life of bitterness. I am reminded of these words from the Gospel of Luke 4:18 (NKJV),

> *"The Spirit of the LORD is upon Me,*
> *Because He has anointed Me*

To preach the gospel to the poor;
He has sent Me to heal the brokenhearted,
To proclaim liberty to the captives
And recovery of sight to the blind,
To set at liberty those who are oppressed…".

The Story Of Paul Elliott

"And in that day, thou shalt say, O Lord, I will praise thee: though thou wast angry with me, thine anger is turned away, and thou comfortedst me.

Behold, God is my salvation; I will trust, and not be afraid: for the Lord Jehovah is my strength and my song; he also is become my salvation.

Therefore, with joy shall ye draw water out of the wells of salvation.

And in that day shall ye say, Praise the Lord, call upon his name, declare his doings among the people, make mention that his name is exalted.

Sing unto the Lord; for he hath done excellent things: this is known in all the earth.

Cry out and shout, thou inhabitant of Zion: for great is the Holy One of Israel in the midst of thee."
Isaiah 12:1-6 (KJV)

Paul Elliott's father, Trevor, was murdered on April 13th, 1983. "A sergeant in the Territorial Army and prominent unionist, he was shot by the IRA as he walked to his car near the shop where he worked in Keady. He was hit seven times by a masked gunman who opened fire at close range as he left the premises in the main street at teatime. The gunman got into a van which drove off towards the Glen Road. The van, stolen in Carrickmacross[75] a fortnight earlier, had been fitted with false number plates and was found abandoned at a derelict house at Mullyash,[76] County Monaghan, close to the border."[77] Trevor was 38 years old; married with five children. The ages of the children, four boys and one girl, were between 7 months and 11 years old.

Before we look further at Paul's story, there are a few background points to mention in regard to this dreadful murder of the shop manager of Powell's grocery store on Main Street in Keady, County Armagh.

Firstly, it demonstrates how porous the border was between Ireland and Northern Ireland. This incident shows how IRA operatives, after committing their crimes in the North could quickly cross the border and find sanctuary in the South of Ireland. This was putting constant pressures on the security services in border areas to protect the families that lived in those communities.

Secondly, Trevor Elliott was a sergeant in the Territorial Army (TA)[78] in Armagh. Following his murder, the TA put out this statement: "We would like to emphasise and stress that we have no connection and no involvement in the security situation here in Northern Ireland."[79] The TA had never been involved in the fight against terrorism. Mr Elliott was the second TA man killed in the Armagh area. On December

---

75 Carrickmacross is a town in County Monaghan, Ireland. This town is about 20miles across the border from Keady, which is in Northern Ireland.
76 Mullyash, County Monaghan, is about 5 miles, across the border, from Keady.
77 McKittrick D., Feeney B., Thornton C. and Kelters S. (1999) "Lost Lives. The stories of the men, women and children who died as a result of the Northern Ireland Troubles", Edinburgh, Mainstream Publishing Company Ltd.
78 The Army Reserve is the active-duty volunteer reserve force of the British Army. It is separate from the Regular Reserve whose members are ex-Regular personnel who retain a statutory liability for service. The Army Reserve was known as the Territorial Force from 1908 to 1921, the Territorial Army (TA) from 1921 to 1967, the Territorial and Army Volunteer Reserve (TAVR) from 1967 to 1979, and again the Territorial Army (TA) from 1979 to 2014. (Wikipedia).
79 McKittrick D., Feeney B., Thornton C. and Kelters S. (1999) "Lost Lives. The stories of the men, women and children who died as a result of the Northern Ireland Troubles", Edinburgh, Mainstream Publishing Company Ltd.

28th, 1980, Sergeant Hugh McGinn was murdered by the INLA. "He answered a knock on his front door at Drumarg Villas in a Republican area of Armagh and two gunmen fired at least twelve rounds, fatally wounding him."[80] These were sectarian murders.

Thirdly, this murder was further evidence of the IRA policy to remove Protestants living in the border areas. Trevor was the press officer for the Armagh branch of the Democratic Unionist Party[81] (DUP). A local unionist councillor said the killing was further evidence of the campaign of genocide mounted against Protestants living in border areas and "a blatant attempt to intimidate the man in the street from taking an active interest in politics."[82] The Protestants in Keady and surrounding area were in the minority.

Fourthly, the murder weapon, an Armalite rifle, had a track record. It had already been used in the murder of a man in February 1983 and, subsequently, it was used in two further murders: one in May and another in June. It seems that the IRA and the INLA both had use of the rifle. So, in a period of four months, this rifle was used to murder two civilians, a policeman and a corporal in the UDR.

Finally, there was a back story and it involved, supposedly, the missing racehorse, Shergar. The horse had been stolen from a stud in County Kildare on February 8, 1983.[83] In those early months of 1983 many searches were undertaken to find the racehorse in Ireland. Plans were in place to search for Shergar along the South

---

80 Burrows S. "From Partition to Peace". County Armagh Phoenix Group Ltd.
81 The Democratic Unionist Party (DUP) is a unionist and loyalist political party in Northern Ireland. It was founded in 1971 during the Troubles by Ian Paisley, who led the party for the next 37 years. (Wikipedia).
82 McKittrick D., Feeney B., Thornton C. and Kelters S. (1999) "Lost Lives. The stories of the men, women and children who died as a result of the Northern Ireland Troubles", Edinburgh, Mainstream Publishing Company Ltd.
83 In 1999, 16 years after the theft, an informer, who had been a member of the IRA in 1983, stated that the republican group had stolen the horse.

Armagh border on the Thursday of the week that Trevor Elliott was murdered. But "Operation Shergar" was, it seems, about more than just looking for a racehorse. In the week of Trevor Elliott's death there had been Republilcan paramilitary activity and British secret services movements going on across the border. Some paramilitaries had been tracked moving south and the security services wanted to sweep the border and create a no man's area. The IRA were aware of these plans. Further, the IRA had said they were ready to launch a new offensive against the security forces and they claimed responsibility for Trevor's killing.

It appeared that a "dirty", tit-for-tat war was going on in the border area. Innocent people were drawn in and caught in the crossfire. I think Trevor Elliott was one such person.

Who was Trevor Elliott?

Trevor's wife was Josephine and they had five children: Deborah, Paul and Gary (twin boys), Jonathan and Stephen.

One of Trevor's sons, in later life, said he thought "the attack on his father was a statement that the type of man his father was did not belong in Keady."

The Rev. Alan Edgar, Minister of Tullyvallen Church, conducting the funeral service paid tribute to the family of Trevor Elliott. He described Trevor as a husband, father, friend and colleague – a loyal son of Ulster and a faithful member of the congregation.

"Trevor Elliott was all of these and more. Born and reared in this city[84] Trevor had established his home in his native town and as a husband

---

[84] Armagh, «the city of saints and scholars», was historically regarded as a city because it was the seat of the Primate of All Ireland.

and father he worked hard to provide for his home and family. Although Trevor has known the risks of running the grocery business in that border town, he had also been involved in part-time farming in south Armagh. He met his death, he was murdered pursuing his chosen calling, that he might support his dependents and today we thank God for a man who believed in the biblical principal that we must earn our bread by the sweat of the brow.

Trevor was not only a family man he was also an Ulster man. He loved his country and he was prepared to put his life on the line for that very reason."

Rev. Edgar described further his role as a part-time sergeant in the TA; his work with the DUP and his drumming with the Army band and Killeen Pipe Band. Rev. Edgar finished his tribute with these words: "We can thank God that Trevor was a born-again believer, a Christian man and we use the term Christian, not in the modern adulterated sense of the word, we use it in its true physical sense.

Eleven years ago, Trevor realised by nature that he was a guilty lost and hell deserving sinner. Thank God he came to Christ in repentance and was washed in the blood of the Lamb and saved by grace. He was a regular attender of this Church especially at the early morning prayer meeting when at 6.30am every Tuesday morning some of the members of this congregation meet together to pray. Last Tuesday morning Trevor Elliott was in the building praying to his Saviour[85] – today he is with his Saviour. We thank God for a man of God.

The family has lost a husband and father, Ulster has lost a loyal son, this congregation has lost a brother in Christ, as we are all the poorer for our loss."[86]

---

85 Trevor Elliott was murdered the next day on Wednesday 13th April 1983.
86 Ulster Gazette and Armagh Standard Thursday 21ˢᵗ April 1983.

Paul Elliott…

Paul was ten years of age when his father was murdered leaving his place of work in Keady. He was carrying a box of groceries, which he was going to deliver to a family on his way home. This was common practice for Paul's father. He was shot at point blank range. At the time of his father's murder, Paul was already home from school and out playing with his brothers, Gary and Jonathan, in the cul-de-sac where the family lived.

The three boys were called into the home of Gary and Lorraine Atkinson, who lived on the same street as the Elliott family. Pastor David Carnduff, who lived in the same cul-de-sac and was the pastor of the local Elim church, met them inside the Atkinson's home. The pastor said to the boys, "Your dad has been shot." Paul asked, "Is he injured or has he died." Pastor Carnduff replied, "Unfortunately, died." The boys then left the house and made their way to their own home. Paul remembers crying as he walked along and passing their neighbours, who were saying, "Very sorry, I'm very sorry." When Paul got to the home there was a lot of commotion. Family, friends and neighbours had gathered. His response was to "straighten himself up". In the hours following, local councillors, TA colleagues and officers, and politicians visited the home to express their shock and condolences. The children spent that evening at home, but then the boys were shared out amongst the family. Paul went to stay with his cousin David.

We must remember that Paul's mother, Josephine, had a seven-month-old baby boy, Stephen, to take care of. One of Trevor's brothers was recorded as saying in regard to his sister-in-law, "His wife is still under heavy sedation. The full horror of the tragedy has not sunk in with her. At this stage we have no idea why he was singled out, but obviously they knew him and knew his movements. It has come as a complete shock."[87]

You might be wondering how a 10-year-old boy had the presence of mind to ask, "Is he injured or has he died?" Paul was a mature boy for his age and fully aware of his surroundings and the Troubles in Northern Ireland. Paul remembered talking with friends, whose fathers were in the UDR. Together they discussed "whose father was the mostly likely to be a target." Paul knew the difference between the responsibilities of UDR personnel and TA volunteers; it was the UDR who patrolled the streets. The friends decided that UDR servicemen were mostly the targets. Paul had seen his friend's father and his own father checking under their vehicles for booby trap bombs. Following his father's murder, an uncle of Paul's had been involved in a booby trap bomb and survived so Paul was fully aware of what was going on in the country and the terrorist threat that Protestant families faced day by day.

In addition to all this, Paul had become a Christian in 1979, at the age of seven. Looking back some forty-two years at the story that unfolded in his life from the age of ten, Paul said, "I was saved at seven to prepare me for the future."

The Elliott home was a Christian home and the family attended the Free Presbyterian Church in Armagh. As well as going to Church on a Sunday, Paul was also attending a weekly children's meeting that was held in a garage in Armagh. Ernie and Ellie Atkinson[88], who belonged to the local Elim church, were the leaders of this Wednesday afternoon outreach to children. Paul remembers this couple as kind

---

87 McKittrick D., Feeney B., Thornton C. and Kelters S. (1999) "Lost Lives. The stories of the men, women and children who died as a result of the Northern Ireland Troubles", Edinburgh, Mainstream Publishing Company Ltd.

88 It was in their son's home where Paul and his brothers were told, by the Elim pastor, that their dad was murdered.

people who were generous in giving prizes as the children learned their Bible memory verses. After giving his heart to the Lord Jesus at one of their meetings, Paul went home and told his sister, Deborah.

Paul said, "My dad was my hero: I loved him and I wanted to do the things that he did. I wanted to be like my father." Paul told us that his father was passionate about his faith. He mentioned how his father could have been on duty all night on a Saturday at the TA barracks but he would be in church on the Sunday morning, sometimes still wearing his TA uniform. Paul also is passionate about his faith. It shone through as he talked about the murder of his father and how he has grown in faith and purpose following that dreadful day April 13th, 1983.

Trevor Elliott was an honest man with a hearty laugh. He enjoyed fun and "the craic"[89]. Paul remembers the family holidays around Newcastle, County Down and the weekly swimming trips in Armagh. His father was a drumming tutor and a very good cook: so much so that he would have done the cooking for "big dinners and 'dos'" for his army colleagues at the TA premises. He was a well-liked and principled man who would speak up if something wasn't right. Paul would have spent time with his father at the TA base. Trevor was in charge of the stores there.

Paul cried at the funeral but then resolved to "step up and take on the role of the man in the house." He took on responsibility. One example was that he did the weekly shopping for the family. Both parents worked prior to the murder of his father. There was a family of seven to provide for. Paul doesn't remember a time when his mother didn't work, either in nursing homes or as a home help. When she returned to work, the arrangement was that Paul would go shopping

---

89 *Craic* is a term for news, gossip, fun, entertainment, and enjoyable conversation, particularly prominent in Ireland. (Wikipedia). "Craic" is Irish and "crack" is Ulster Scots.

in Armagh at 4.30pm on a Saturday and either walk home or his mother would pick him up at 5.30pm, on her return from work. The children were never left without child care when their mother was working, but Paul did the shopping and he would go from shop to shop buying meat, bread, fruit and veg for the week. His reward was that he was given money to buy a football magazine. He also did other jobs around the house, such as cutting the grass and washing the car and the dishes.

He said, "I kept busy. I coped just by getting on with it. I didn't wallow in self-pity. They had made a victim out of my father, but not me." Of course, Paul missed his father, but he didn't allow himself to think too much: "I knew he was gone. There was sadness that he wasn't here, but I didn't pine. I remembered him very fondly. I wanted to make him proud"

There have been occasions since the death of his father when he has missed him particularly, such as birthdays, passing his driving test, his wedding and when his children were born. However, Paul had a resolve – keep busy, help his mother and siblings and keep following his Lord and Saviour, Jesus Christ.

Tribute should be paid here to Paul's mother, Josephine. When her husband was murdered, Josephine was 32 years old. She was a widow with five children; the youngest was seven months old. Within a year, a new house was purchased. She returned to work and continued to attend the Free Presbyterian Church. She had her own grief to carry but also five children to provide and care for. Paul said, "The children kept her going. She had to." She was a remarkably strong and resolute mother. The Bible tells us that the Lord defends the widow. Undoubtedly Josephine could witness to the truth of this promise from the Scriptures.

Paul mentioned how each member of the family had their own struggles but they helped each other. The wider family circle provided constant support and came around the family, including Uncle Ivan, who called at the house most days.

Although his father had been murdered, Paul still attended various children's meetings each week and his own church on a Sunday. He made the effort; "I wanted to go to these meetings. God was in my heart." It is remarkable for a ten-year boy, who had experienced the loss of his father, that his desires toward God are firm and strong. Paul is very honest and says that there were times when his faith waned but he was aware that God was holding on to him and that He never left him. A verse of scripture that became real as time went by was Matthew 5:4: *"Blessed are they that mourn; for they shall be comforted."* (KJV). Paul said, "The Lord comforted me daily; I asked for strength on a daily basis."

In the years that followed the death of his father, Paul witnessed how God surrounded the family and himself with Christian people. There were five churches in particular in Armagh which helped the family: their own church: The Free Presbyterian Church, The Mall Presbyterian Church, the Elim Pentecostal Church, the Baptist Church and Milford Christian Fellowship. There are two stories to mention:

Paul told of how the local Baptist church "bent over backwards" to help the family purchase another property in Armagh. The family moved to this new home within a year of Trevor's murder. Paul commented, "My mother made a good decision in purchasing this house". It was a new start for the family and a local church made it possible.

The second story is about Milford Christian Fellowship, a Brethren assembly. In his early teens, Paul started to attend the youth meetings and the Lord brought a man into his life called David Wilson. "He was my pastor and a constant figure in my life. He stepped up and prayed for me. He was like a father figure for me. He helped me to go on following the Lord." Paul mentioned that David promised he would give £10.00 as a prize for anyone who could recite Isaiah chapter 53. "I made sure that I knew it. There was method in this. It was a way of teaching us to hide God's word so that we would not sin against the Lord: *"Thy word have I hid in mine heart, that I might not sin against thee."* Psalm 119:11 (KJV).

Paul is not a bitter man. No one was ever charged with the murder of his father and his answer to the question, "Are you disappointed?", was "No." On one occasion Paul was giving his testimony at a church in Belfast. At the end of the service someone asked him, "Why are you not bitter? How have you dealt with the bitterness?" His answer was, "I didn't deal with it, God did." He is honest in saying that the removing of bitterness has been a process but that the LORD has been faithful and present in this work of grace in his heart.

Paul has an unshakable faith and trust in the LORD God. He knows that God is sovereign and in control and that, without any sense of revenge or pleasure, there is a judgment to come when all will stand before the Lord to answer for their deeds, their words and their thoughts. What is Paul's life now? He quoted these words from Isaiah 61:3: *"To appoint unto them that mourn in Zion, to give unto them beauty for ashes, the oil of joy for mourning, the garment of praise for the spirit of heaviness; that they might be called trees of righteousness, the planting of the* LORD, *that he might be glorified."* (KJV).

In 2006 Paul experienced an answer to prayer that taught him an important lesson. Paul's wife, Liza, was not a Christian but was not antagonistic to Paul's faith. He was asked, by his local church fellowship, to get involved in the Summer Holiday Bible Club week. It was suggested that perhaps Liza would also like to come with him to help out. Liza, did go, and on the Thursday evening, she became a follower of the LORD Jesus. The lesson Paul learned was this: if you demonstrate a desire to do something for the LORD and step out, then He will step in and show what He can do.

Another occasion when Paul stepped out for the LORD was on the thirty-year anniversary of the murder of his father. Along with his family, Paul decided it was the right time to remember and honour his father with a special anniversary event. This event proved pivotal in his life. Paul said that it "brought closure" for him.

In the thirty years, prior to 2013 on the tenth and twentieth anniversaries, the family didn't feel the time was right for them to speak out publicly in honour of their father. Although they didn't have any fear about coming out publicly to speak about him, they didn't want to draw attention to the family. However, since his murder, Trevor Elliott is remembered every year on the July 12th, at an annual Remembrance Service in Armagh.

For the thirtieth anniversary, Paul and his family, stepped out in two ways:

Firstly, because Paul's father was a drumming tutor and played the drums for the TA pipe band, a Lambeg[90] drum, with a picture of his father on the drum frame, was commissioned and dedicated in honour of his death.

Secondly, a local hall was hired and past colleagues and associates of Trevor's, along with family and friends, were invited to a Gospel evening, where Trevor's life would be celebrated. Paul's minister gave a short, relevant Gospel message and Paul shared his father's testimony. The key question asked of those gathered was, "Do you know Trevor Elliott's Saviour?" The blessing of the evening was that one of Paul's

---

90 A Lambeg drum is a large drum, beaten with curved malacca canes. It is used primarily in Northern Ireland by Unionists and the Orange Order traditionally in street parades held in the summer, particularly on and around 12th July («The Twelfth"). (Wikipedia).

brothers, Jonathan, and his wife, came to faith in the LORD Jesus Christ a short time after the event. Thirty years, after Trevor's death, his legacy was still bearing fruit. Paul spoke the scripture, "God is the rewarder of those who diligently seek him." The Bible teaches us that if there is sin hiding in our hearts then the LORD will not answer our prayers. The blessing that Paul experienced following this Gospel event in his father's honour, is an indication that there was no bitterness or spirit of revenge in his heart which would have displeased the LORD.

As Paul got older, he realised that there were local organisations that he could join where perhaps he could avenge his father's murder. He resisted the temptation to become involved in a more sinister fight against terrorism and instead has gone on the serve the Lord in the Lord's army. "God sets you free to forgive," Paul said. The scripture Paul quoted was from the Psalms, "God is a refuge and strength." Since the event in 2013 to celebrate his father's life, Paul believes, "God's blessing has flowed in a greater way" upon his life and ministry. This demonstrates again how, as we step out for the Lord, He will step in and reveal who He is and what He can do.

In the years since April 2013, doors have opened for Paul to go to different churches and to the band's fraternity and mission events all over Northern Ireland to sing the Gospel message and share his testimony. He comments, "If I didn't have the testimony of a victim, would I be asked? No, I don't think so." To Paul's credit, he uses every opportunity to speak about his love for his Saviour. He lives and breathes the Gospel. He has a passion to share his testimony: "I want people to see Christ in me. He has been the one who has carried me through. I live with the joy of the Lord in my heart."

Paul has also drawn alongside many people who have lost someone precious in their lives, encouraging them to talk about their loss and ask the difficult questions we would all ask if faced with tragic circumstances. He is able to bring care and compassion and the Gospel into the situation, because of his own experience.

Paul is not a bitter man or a vengeful man or a man with a "chip on his shoulder". He certainly doesn't see himself as a victim. There is no strident call for justice. This demand, found in certain quarters in Northern Ireland on both sides of the religious divide, is not eating away in his heart and mind. Actually, Paul said, "I don't need justice to live my life". He believes that ultimate justice is in God's hands. He doesn't want to be revictimised. Paul tells how a few years ago he was offered counselling by Government agencies. He had been critical, over the years, of the lack of such intervention for the victims. He went to the sessions because he felt it would have been hypocritical not to have gone, after being critical of the lack of counselling support. Paul said, "The course revictimised me. I woke up with nightmares. I couldn't sleep if anything about the past came up on the news." His desire, now, is to live for God and be a blessing to his family.

"Was God angry with me?" Paul said in regard to his father's murder. "I never thought that. God is angry with me but that is because of my own sin. If my father was living today would Liza, Jonathan and his wife be saved? Sometimes there has to be sacrifice. Yes, I would want my father to be still with me but would I have had the opportunity to talk about my father's faith and my faith? It has taken time, but God has opened up a ministry for me. I don't blame God. I go another way. He strengthens me."

There are two Biblical truths Paul is very certain about:

Firstly, he will see his father again. "I will see him when I walk through the door of heaven." The Apostle Paul, in the New Testament, tells us that Christians don't mourn as the world mourns the loss of someone because of the hope we have in the Lord Jesus.

Secondly, vengeance belongs to God. Paul quoted this Bible verse from Romans 12:19: *"Dearly beloved, avenge not yourselves, but rather give place unto wrath: for it is written, Vengeance is mine; I will repay, saith the Lord."* (KJV). (see also Deuteronomy 32:35). Although no one was charged with the murder of Trevor Elliott there was local knowledge about those who were involved in the killing.

The Apostle Paul writes, quoting from Isaiah 54:17, *"No weapon that is formed against thee shall prosper; and every tongue that shall rise against thee in judgment thou shalt condemn. This is the heritage of the servants of the* LORD, *and their righteousness is of me, saith the* LORD.*"* (KJV). The suspected culprit in the death of Trevor Elliott died a violent death and some members of the person's family also died violently and suddenly. One of those who died, was 38 years of age with five children; exactly the age of Trevor, who had five children. Paul said, that God does take a dealing with people. That is the promise of Isaiah 54:17. Paul is not a spiteful or vengeful person, but seeks to live and serve according to God's Word.

At the beginning of this chapter, Isaiah 12:1-6 (KJV) is quoted.

> *"And in that day, thou shalt say, O* LORD, *I will praise thee: though thou wast angry with me, thine anger is turned away, and thou comfortedst me. Behold, God is my salvation; I will trust, and not be afraid: for the* LORD JEHOVAH *is my strength and my song; he also is become my salvation. Therefore, with joy shall ye draw water out of the wells of salvation. And in that day shall ye say, Praise the* LORD, *call upon his name, declare his doings among the people, make mention that his name is exalted. Sing unto the* LORD; *for he hath done excellent things: this is known in all the earth. Cry out and shout, thou inhabitant of Zion: for great is the Holy One of Israel in the midst of thee."*

These were the Scriptures that Paul wanted to head up the chapter on his life. They are very special verses for him because they sum up his testimony.[91] He says this in regard to verse 6, "Since my salvation, the Holy One has been in my midst – in shock and sickness."

This was the third attack on these premises during the years of the Troubles. On the thirtieth anniversary of Trevor Elliott's death, Paul challenged the group that was gathered with these words, "Do you know Trevor Elliott's Saviour?"

You have read Paul's story, and the challenge is this: "Do you know Paul Elliott's Saviour?"

---

91 See www.sermonaudio.com/solo/armaghfpc/sermons/11120212722689/

The Story Of Sara-Louise Martin

"Then the LORD said, 'My Spirit will not contend with humans forever, for they are mortal; their days will be a hundred and twenty years.'"
Genesis 6:3 (NIV)

Sara-Louise is the daughter of Inspector Brian Martin. On November 4th, 1983, she lost her father in a bomb attack on the Ulster Polytechnic at Jordanstown, Belfast.

This was the first of three attacks on these premises during the years of the Troubles. The last was on March 24th, 1977. "A bomb exploded without warning in a crowded lecture hall ... injuring 10 persons, including the 80-year-old former Lord Justice of Ulster, Lord MacDermott ... A young lecturer was seriously injured in the chest and head by the four-pound bomb, which exploded under the platform throwing fragments of wood and metal in all directions in the hall of the Ulster Polytechnic."[92] Police believed that Lord MacDermott was the intended target.

Of all the attacks on the Ulster Polytechnic, the bombing on November 4th, 1983 was the first one involving fatalities.

The Belfast Telegraph gave this report that day in their evening edition: "A policeman was killed and more than 30 people injured

---

92 New York Times 25th March 1977

when a bomb exploded in a lecture room at the Ulster Polytechnic at Jordanstown today. Four of the injured were RUC men who were attending a class for their Higher National Certificate, when the no-warning blast ripped through the building. This afternoon three policemen were in intensive care with very serious injuries. One other was described as 'comfortable.' Five others were discharged after treatment and several more were still in hospital with minor injuries. None of the civilians was seriously hurt. The bomb blew out a wall in the third-storey classroom killing the man instantly and injuring many of his colleagues."[93]

The RUC officers were on a day-release course in police studies. The same room was used every Friday for the class and fourteen of the thirty who were injured were police officers.

On the November 5th, 1983, there was this updated report of the attack: "The IRA used a shrapnel bomb to kill two policemen in the Ulster Polytechnic at Jordanstown, it was revealed today. The two pounds of gelignite was packed with bolts and nails and hidden in the roof space above the lecture room. It is believed a sophisticated electronic timing system was used to automatically arm the bomb and then detonate the explosives."[94]

Inspector Brian Martin died at the entrance of Accident and Emergency at the Royal Victoria Hospital, Belfast, on Friday November 4th, 1983, and Sergeant Stephen Fyffe died later that day. Sergeant William McDonald, also fatally wounded, died nine months later.

"The sociology lecturer taking the class at Jordanstown said, 'I received a stunning blow to the right side of my head. I heard no sound. I

---

[93] Belfast Telegraph 4th November 1983
[94] Belfast Telegraph 5th November 1983

began to sink to the floor. I could see nothing. Within seconds I was kneeling. I could just see debris and dust."[95]

"Officials said there was no warning before the bomb detonated near the professor's lectern in a criminology class at Ulster Polytechnic, ripping through the classroom and dumping wall masonry onto the students. 'I heard a massive bang and then the wall fell on top of me,' said one student before he was whisked off in an ambulance to be treated for shock. 'Lots of the others didn't stand a chance. Some of them had their arms and legs blown off. It was terrible. I couldn't stay to help.' More than two dozen students in adjoining classrooms of the Polytechnic were taken to hospitals to be treated for shock."[96]

Later in the day on Friday November 4th, a car bomb wrecked a bar in Strabane, 60 miles west of Belfast. This bar was frequented by off-duty policemen. In answer to a question Rev. William McCrea put to James Prior, the Secretary of State for Northern Ireland, about this bombing, we gleaned these details about the attack:

"At 9.59 pm on Friday November 4th, 1983, an explosion occurred in a van which had been left in the middle of Patrick Street, Strabane outside the Fair bar. No warning had been given. The Irish National Liberation Army subsequently claimed responsibility. The explosion demolished the bar and severely damaged two nearby dwellings. Fourteen private dwellings and a licensed restaurant suffered extensive damage and 38 other buildings in the surrounding area suffered lesser damage. A number of vehicles were also damaged. Thirteen people including three policemen were seriously injured and were admitted to Altnagelvin hospital, Londonderry. Another 16 people were also hurt but did not require admission to hospital."

---

[95] McKittrick D., Feeney B., Thornton C. and Kelters S. (1999) "Lost Lives. The stories of the men, women and children who died as a result of the Northern Ireland Troubles", Edinburgh, Mainstream Publishing Company Ltd.

[96] See www.upi.com/Archives

What was behind these two IRA attacks on the RUC in Northern Ireland? The opinion among politicians and the security services was that the IRA were giving a warning shot because of the Anglo-Irish talks that were planned in London the following week.

The Martin Family...

Brian was 28 years of age when he was murdered by the IRA. He was married to Iris, who was pregnant with their second child, John. They already had one child, Sara-Louise. She was 13 months old.

Brian, originally from Rathfriland, lived with his family in Banbridge. He was stationed in Portadown.

Who was Inspector Brian Martin?

Brian was a Christian and wrote his testimony in a tract that was published in the year of his death,1983. It was called "The Saving and Keeping Power – the Testimony of Inspector John Brian Martin (1955-1983). Brian wrote:

"The Lord brought me into the world on the 4th December 1955 and the earliest recollection I have is when I was very small and my father getting down on his knees with me at night before I went to bed and reciting the Lord's Prayer to me until I was able to say it as well. I was the eldest in a family of three, having two younger sisters.

I was not raised in a Christian home but in 'a church home'. I was taken to Sunday school and church every Sunday and was even encouraged to do scripture exams. Then, when I was 11 years old, my father died. This had a profound effect on me at the time, as I was the eldest in the family. To my mother's credit, she saw to it that I still attended Sunday school, church and the Youth Club.

At 18, I joined the Police and it was while training at Enniskillen that I first came into contact with the Christian Police Association, as they distributed a copy of the New Testament to each recruit. Back then I had more concern for the things of the world than my own soul; cars and having a good time were all I was concerned about.

I was by no means a drunkard but drink to me then seemed to be the 'in thing' socially as it appeared to have some sort of status attached to it. I continued in this vein of life and then got married. Just before I got married my wife became a Christian. She told me at the time and I can remember thinking distastefully about her decision. Now I can see that this was part of God's plan for me. I went to church as regularly as possible, was a choir member, a committee member and even went along with my wife to the mid-week Bible study and prayer meeting. I had the outward appearance of being a Christian but still I knew I had not made the commitment that was required.

I went to various missions and gospel halls with my wife and at the beginning of 1980 I knew the Lord was talking to me. I was confused and restless and feeling extremely agitated. My wife and her mother, both committed Christians, I knew were praying for my salvation. I knew within myself what I had to do, but pride in myself was keeping me from doing so.

Finally, on May 18th, 1981, after attending a gospel service in Rathfriland the previous evening, I committed my life to the Lord. I went to see my own minister that day, seeking for salvation, counsel and guidance. I felt very humbled in this but the Lord gave me courage to do it. I spent a gratifying time with my minister that morning and after making a simple prayer with him and commitment, I felt all the unrest and unease begin to lessen. We both spent a time of fellowship together and, when I went to work that evening, I told a colleague (who I knew was a committed Christian) of my experience, which helped me in my stand. At that moment I was at peace within myself and had an assurance which I never had before. I wondered how I might tell some of my non-Christian friends. This was made easy for me with the Lord's help.

I can say in all honesty that to lead a Christian life, especially in the Police Force, is not an easy one. It is a battlefield all the way, but although not an easy life, it is a blessed life. If you, dear friend, are holding back from commitment to the Lord because of your own pride, as was my case, I would say to you, act now before it is too late. In Genesis 6:3 it says that *'the Lord's Spirit shall not always strive with man'*.

This indeed is a sobering thought. If you feel that the Lord is talking to you and you are under conviction, I would urge you to act; the Christian life, as I have found every day, brings a new challenge, a new experience and new friends."[97]

I understand that Brian put his testimony in print only a short time before his murder in November 1983. He had been a Christian for only 2 years and 5 months.

The Funeral of Inspector Brian Martin…

Over three-thousand people attended the funeral of Brian Martin. It was the largest funeral the town had ever witnessed. The service in the church was relayed to an overflow congregation in the church hall and to others who stood in the church grounds.

---

97 Sourced – Elizabeth Burke's Blog

The local minister, Rev. William Sanderson, said that his first reaction on hearing of the murder of Brian "was one of intense anger against those who carried out such a foul deed but that anger had given way to pity for those who were so evil, so depraved and so misguided.

He hoped those responsible would be brought to justice and he asked that none of the hatred or bitterness, which has been the cause of such … in the province would follow the officer's murder."

Brian was a member of the Christian Police Association and they took part in the service.

Sara-Louise…

Pat and I were unable to meet up with Sara-Louise face to face to hear her story, which is a regret. Perhaps, one day, we will be able to remedy that. As a substitute, we gave Sara-Louise some questions as guidance to help tell her story following the murder of her father, Inspector Brian Martin. We really appreciate what Sara-Louise was able to put in writing.

What was your Life like prior to the Tragic Event?

"I was a baby when my father was murdered. It happened 18 days after my first birthday. My mum was also 6 weeks pregnant with my brother John at the time. My dad knew about the pregnancy (and was overjoyed). Apparently, his exact words were 'the more the merrier' but no one in the family knew that Mum was pregnant at the time of Dad's murder.

I have no memories of my father but I understand from other people that we shared a close bond. My Mum had become a Christian a few years before Dad was murdered and Dad had also come to faith a couple of years prior to his murder."

Iris, Brian's wife, was now widowed, with a young daughter of 13 months, and carrying their second child: there was still another 8 months before this child was born. We can imagine the heartbreak and the questions that must have engulfed Iris as she cared for Sara-Louise and watched for the day when John was born. There was no husband to celebrate with and there was no father to care and lead the family. This young Christian family experienced the most tragic of circumstances.

How did you Suffer?

"I don't have any vivid memories of what happened at the time, I was a small baby. I have taken a keen interest in early child development and understand that at 13 months old I would have been aware of my father being there one day and then vanishing the next. I understand that this would be very confusing for a small baby, particular with a close care-giver.

My father's murder has cast a very long shadow over my life and the life of all impacted by his murder. My father was stolen from me. Stolen from all of us. Snatched away in the prime of his life. He was doing really well in his career as a policeman – he was the youngest ever policeman to reach the rank of Inspector and had a full and promising career ahead of him.

My early childhood years were really happy. My mum is an incredibly nurturing woman and surrounded us with love and affection. I was always fully aware of what happened to my dad and yet Mum did a wonderful job of bringing us up in a way that named what had happened to us, but didn't let it define us? We have a really tightly knit extended family and group of church friends who were so kind to us, inviting us to be part of their lives, holidays and every day."

Pat and I spoke to a number of Christian people about the traumatic experiences they suffered during the Troubles. The one abiding memory we have is this: how each person sought to respond without seeking revenge. Iris is an example of this. She didn't want her children to live in a prison house of bitterness. She was honest. The facts were stated but there was no suggestion of living for revenge. She knew that forgiveness was the only way that we would live in freedom.

What Cost did you Experience?

"Growing up without a father is a hard thing. Missing out on the fatherly affirmation, security and safety provided in a fatherly relationship was hard. I don't think I really dealt with any of it properly until I was in my early 30's. My father's murder investigation was re-opened. I think the biggest impact that it's had on my life is a general feeling of 'feeling a bit lost' most of the time – kind of a bit detached from things or not always really getting fully involved, hesitant. That's how I felt internally a lot of the time. I may have appeared to be different externally, confident sometimes, but that's how I felt inside for a big chunk of my life.

Reflecting on it all now, and all the inner work that I've done in recent years, I can see that it had a big impact on my identity. I so desperately needed my life story to be more than 'my dad got murdered and life is crap as a consequence' – it was really crap at times, but I also knew that a different story was possible and I was on an absolute mission to make that happen."

Sara-Louise has written honestly about the cost that she suffered for over thirty years, following the murder of her father. It is difficult for us to understand the "dark periods" that she must have gone through in those years. She has clearly demonstrated courage in facing life without a father and seeking to live "a different story" to that of a victim.

Your Early thoughts?

"When I was much younger, I had a very simple understanding of what it all meant. It's only been in recent years, when I've looked at things through a historical and political lens, that I have seen it in a different way.

There were a lot of searching prayers which often repeated the 'Why did this have to happen?' My biggest faith struggle has always been 'Is God really good? Can I trust Him? Does He actually want good things for me?' My experience did not demonstrate that God was good. My experience was one of loss and pain and confusion.

I think the biggest fear that I had was that something would happen to my mum and THEN what would I do? I can remember worrying about that a lot as a child and teenager. I think that my subconscious way of dealing with that was to be as practically-minded as possible, so that if the worst did happen, I would be okay."

How did Christians Help?

"When we were very small, there were a number of families at church that really supported us and included us in their family life. I think Mum was quite well supported by our church family in those early years too. There have definitely been people who have gone the distance, supporting us up to the present day. Those people are very special. That faithful support has really impacted me and my life.

People who you can count on are a rare breed. I think it's really impacted how I see friendship and how I want to invest in people. God's love in action really can change lives. It's changed mine.

There have been people who have encouraged me over the years. When someone has a history of loving and supporting you, you're more likely to allow them to speak into your life when things are tough – they have gone the distance.

There were people who slipped me bible verses. In my teens and twenties when I was trying to figure out what to do with my life, there were people who prayed me through various transitions."

The Martin family attended a Presbyterian church in the locality where they lived. I have already mentioned the book "Considering Grace": a book which interviewed 120 people from the Presbyterian church, about their traumatic experiences in the Troubles. The book is honest: the response of some local churches in helping victims could have been better handled at times. Thank God for the Christians at the Presbyterian church where the Martin family belonged. Brian was in the church choir and fulfilled an administrative role in the church. Individuals in and around Sara-Louise's life went the distance with her. They have stood by her from childhood to teens to adulthood, by prayer and sharing encouraging and comforting words from the Bible.

Where were You in Your Thinking?

"It is only really very recently that I can, hand on heart, say that I believe that God is good. For the majority of my life the biggest question that I have been trying to unpack is 'Is God good?'. From my experience, it didn't look like it. I was hungry and curious and pursued that question in various different ways.

I searched the scripture and was so relieved to find out that so much of the Psalms were 'laments'. I have been so weary and disappointed with God and I also felt bad about that ... which made it worse.

I just couldn't understand why everything seemed to work out so easily for everyone else and why it felt like I was wading through treacle the majority of the time. God got my anger and that felt good. It was also disappointing. I would say that disappointment has been the most familiar feeling to me as I try to work this all out.

Disappointment is heavy. It's only been in recent years when I have done more 'inner work' that I have unpacked this all in more detail and separated out what is biblical and true and what's a distortion of 'the enemy' to keep me distracted and away from all that God has stored up for me precisely because HE IS GOOD."

Sara-Louise mentions the laments that she found in the Psalms. Someone has said that lamenting is the Christian way to grieve. God has included these laments in the Bible for us to use in our griefs and in the midst of our valleys. Thank God that Sara-Louise found these grief-filled songs and, like so many others, found them to be meaningful in the depths of her disappointments.

What Path has your Life taken since the Tragedy?

"One of the things that's been a big part of my life is the urge to want to make a positive difference in the world. For so much of my life that entailed being involved in lots of things at my church. In more recent years I have been able to integrate that into the work that I do through the small company that I co-founded a few years ago, called Impact Central."

Suffering and the Christian faith...

"Suffering is part of the Christian walk. The bible is a book FULL of stories of people who suffered – of people who questioned God because of their suffering. Of people who rejoiced in their pain because they knew that all could be redeemed through God.

To be a person of faith means that you will suffer. Days can be hard. We want mountaintop moments but we live a lot of our lives in the valleys and the ascent out of the valleys. Something that a friend said to me many years ago has stuck with me 'We impress with our strengths, but we connect through our vulnerabilities'. To be able to share what God has done in my life and demonstrate that he can redeem a horrendous situation is a privilege. My 30's have been a really tough decade and will be known as the 'Job' decade. So much loss. So much disappointment. So much pain. But I survived.

God has done a deep healing work in me during this decade. I've been completely stripped back. I had an encounter with someone linked to what happened to my dad, just a number of weeks ago that was profoundly healing. I'm stepping into my 40's with joy and expectation that the best is yet to come. All glory to God for his faithfulness!"

Thank God for the honesty and openness that Sara-Louise has revealed in this story. "Suffering is part of the Christian walk," writes Sara-Louise. One of the aims of this book is to challenge the hype and the promotional material that Christians are bombarded with from many platforms: "Come to God and you will have a good life"; "Come to God and he will give you the best." I believe that there is an overcoming, abundant life presented to us in the New Testament, but I also see the message of suffering: God uses suffering to weed out of our lives agendas and motives that are selfish and self-serving.

"Then the LORD said, 'My Spirit will not contend with humans forever, for they are mortal.'" Genesis 6:3 (NIV)

This was the verse of Scripture that Inspector Brian Martin included in his testimony leaflet, written only a short time before his murder. What was in Brian's heart when he quoted this verse?

I believe his passion was to listen to the voice of God and to yield to His judgements in our lives; judgements regarding our selfish ways of living; judgements regarding our sinful motives and thoughts. Peter tells us that *"God is longsuffering to us-ward, not willing that any should perish, but that all should come to repentance."* 2 Peter 3:9.

God doesn't just sit in Heaven judging and condemning us and keeping his distance from us. God is working by the Holy Spirit to draw us to Himself.

Brian's appeal in his testimony leaflet is still relevant today:

"If you dear friend, are holding back from commitment to the Lord because of your own pride, as was my case, I would say to you, act now before it is too late. In Genesis 6:3 it says that the Lord's Spirit shall not always strive with man.

This indeed is a sobering thought. If you feel that the Lord is talking to you and you are under conviction, I would urge you to act; the Christian life, as I have found every day, brings a new challenge, a new experience and new friends."

The Story Of Maggie Burrows

"You intended to harm me, but God intended it for good to accomplish what is now being done, the saving of many lives."
Genesis 50:20.

On March 3rd, 1984, Maggie Burrow's brother-in-law, Herbert (Herbie) Burrows, was killed by an "IRA bomb attached to the door at the firm where he worked. He was blown over a wall and thrown 25 yards by the force of the blast. The device went off when he opened the side door to polish a limousine for a wedding. The IRA said his killing was not an accident and claimed he was a serving member of the UDR, but this was denied by the police and army."[98]

The explosion happened at 10.20am and demolished the building. A booby-trap device had been attached to the door and it was triggered as the side door was opened. The device was planted by the second battalion of the IRA's North Armagh Brigade.

The Rector of St. Mark's Parish Church, Rev. John Batchelor, stated at the funeral, "In spite of any statements from the IRA the killing of

---

98 McKittrick D., Feeney B., Thornton C. and Kelters S. (1999) "Lost Lives. The stories of the men, women and children who died as a result of the Northern Ireland Troubles", Edinburgh, Mainstream Publishing Company Ltd.

Herbert Burrows was no mistake. Someone gathered the information and arranged and planted the device that was to cost him his life."[99]

This murder was condemned by many from across the political and religious sections of Northern Ireland society. The Ulster Gazette, in reporting the bombing, included this contribution from Father Denis Faul: "Dungannon priest, Fr. Denis Faul, said the Catholic community was filled with revulsion at the murders of both Mr Burrows and Castlederg UDR man, Mr Thomas Loughlin.[100] But, he said that the community had been intimidated so much by the IRA and the INLA that they were afraid to take effective action to put an end to the murders in their midst. And he continued: "This 'bomb to kill' policy of the Provisional IRA is more murderous and immoral than the 'shoot to kill' policy which has been criticised in recent months.'" It is worth mentioning that the IRA and INLA were also vicious, at times, toward the Catholic community.

Herbie was 37 years old at the time of his murder. He was an innocent victim and had no links to the security services in Northern Ireland.

Who was Herbie Burrows?

Herbie was married to Barbara but this wasn't the first time that the family had suffered at the hands of the IRA. On October 26th, 1976, Barbara's father, Joseph Wilson, was murdered at his work in Armagh (see chapter 9). At the time of this shooting Barbara was pregnant with her first child, David. When Herbie was killed, there was a second child in the family, Stephen.[101]

---

99 The Ulster Gazette, also known as the Ulster Gazette and Armagh Standard is a newspaper based in Armagh, Northern Ireland, UK. (Wikipedia):

100 Mr Thomas Louglin: murdered on 2nd March 1984 by a booby trap bomb planted by the IRA under his Department of Environment van.

101 David was aged 7 and Stephen was aged 5 when their father was murdered.

Herbie, with a friend, Jackson Stoops, had bought Leathem Funeral Services in 1980. The offices and garage were located on Alexander Road, Armagh. These premises were on the edge of the mainly Catholic Banbrook Hill, Drumbreda area of Armagh and, at that time, Herbie and his business partner were looking for alternative premises in the town.

A local paper gave these insights into Herbie Burrows:

"At 37 he was a man with a deep sense of community spirit and an endless worker for charitable causes."[102]

"Herbie Burrows … was a God-fearing Christian of the highest repute, a family man loved by all who knew him."[103]

Herbie previously told his minister, Rev. John Batchelor, that he didn't want his name on his coffin "as long as my name in in the Lamb's Book of Life."[104] As Maggie, his sister-in-law said, "Herbie was ready to go." Herbie had come to faith in the Lord Jesus a short time before his death.

Barbara, Herbie's wife, and Maggie were best friends and they married identical twin brothers: Barbara married Herbie and Maggie married Stanley.

Maggie related something of her family's story prior to the incident in March 1984 and of her experience after the murder of her brother-in-law.

---

102 Ulster Gazette

103 Ulster Gazette

104 "Lamb's book of Life" – Revelation 21:27 "And there shall in no wise enter into it any thing that defileth, neither whatsoever worketh abomination, or maketh a lie: but they which are written in the Lamb's book of life." (KJV).

Maggie Burrow's Family...

"I had been married to Stanley for six years. We had two boys and so did Herbie and Barbara. Stanley and I had lived in a housing executive house and had just bought our first home. Home life was good, and we were excited to move into our new house. Our boys were very close to Herbie's. My oldest boy and Herbie's youngest boy attended the same local primary school.

We had just bought our new home a year previously and were doing renovations to it. We were putting in a new plumbing system and, because of that, we had moved in with Herbie, Barbara and their two boys about four weeks previously. We had gotten on well sharing their 3 bedded semi-detached home, despite being cramped. We had a very special time of which, looking back, we were thankful.

Stanley and I were brought up Church of Ireland (C.O.I.), and, after we had been married, we attended my family church regularly. I had been brought up in the church we attended, was involved in church organisations, was baptized and confirmed and was a regular communicant. Although church was important to us, neither of us were born-again Christians.

Stanley and I were keen mountain walkers and camped regularly up the Mourne Mountains with the boys. We both loved to jog and took part in 10k runs together. I was a keen dressmaker and Stanley loved to build model aircraft. We became keen gardeners when we purchased our own home.

Stanley was a grocer by trade and had been in partnership with his friend[105] in a rural grocery shop. He left the shop under threat and joined the UDR full-time. I was a practice nurse in a rural surgery."

---

105 Friend was Trevor Elliott – see chapter 4

The Day of the Bomb...

"On the morning of March 3rd, 1984, Stanley was helping our plumber in our home when he received a phone call from his office informing him there had been an explosion in the location where his brother Herbie had his undertaking business. He left our home and went to the premises where the explosion had taken place under Herbie's wedding car. He witnessed the mutilation of his twin's body. I had received a phone call to my place of work from my brother to say that Herbie had been blown up. Stanley and my brother came out to collect me from work. The shock and trauma of the event left us reeling and devastated. We were plunged into unspeakable grief. The fact that Herbie was blown up in a case of mistaken identity left us feeling guilty, remorseful and a whole plethora of mixed feelings, we struggled to even identify and understand the enormity of the situation."

The Cost and the Questions...

"The family was completely turned upside down. Our children were young as were Herbie's and navigating the fears, questions and worries of children while grieving ourselves was a difficult journey for us all. One of my children had a recurring nightmare of black gloved hands and the other wanted to take a ladder to heaven to bring uncle Herbie back. Whilst our extended families all pulled together, there was a feeling of emptiness in the deep grief. Survivor's guilt was something felt by both Stanley and me."

These two families were very close. They had helped each other with child-care as required with working schedules. They had spent time together having fun and family times. Maggie's oldest son, Neil, on being told of his uncle's death, wanted to go and see his Auntie Barbara. Maggie didn't know what to do for the best. On the advice of Maggie's mother, Neil went to see his aunt just after the funeral: "He went into the home and went to sit on his auntie's knee. Barbara had a nickname for Neil – 'he was her Nellie'. He just sat, without saying anything on his auntie's knee, without moving." One can only imagine what comfort this brought Barbara's heart.

Maggie wrote, "Stanley fought terrorism to the hilt but we didn't place the blame on the Catholic community but on the terrorists who carried out the atrocity. I was acutely aware of man's propensity for evil but I did not have a feeling of blame towards God.

The comfort I experienced was the love and support from my immediate family and friends as well as fellow victims of terrorism. Our Rector was very supportive in visitation and reading the scriptures.

A lot of emotions were locked in because of the enormity of it all, especially survivor's guilt. We chose to carry on the best we could but didn't necessarily discuss our feelings of grief and loss. However, I certainly experienced the different stages of grief as I tried to internally process all that had happened, whereas Stanley shut down and could not talk about his twin brother."

Stanley was full-time in the UDR. By the time of the slaughter of his twin brother, he had personally experienced 40 of his own men killed by republican terrorists in separate incidents. He had attended every one of those incidents and been to every funeral. Only 11 months prior to the murder of his twin brother, Stanley's friend and previous business partner, Trevor Elliott, had been killed. In a book that Stanley produced[106] he wrote about the mental suffering that families experienced when a family member left home to go on duty with the UDR, RUC or other security forces. Maggie, Stanley's wife,

---

106 Burrows S. "From Partition to Peace". County Armagh Phoenix Group Ltd.

and the wider family circle, would have known this suffering every time Stanley went off to serve with the UDR.

Stanley wrote further, "They suffered even more when that terrible knock came on their door with the news of the death of a loved one." However, it wasn't a knock on the door for Stanley, but a phone call alerting him to the incident at his brother's workplace. Maggie said, "It was a devasting time for the family. We couldn't make sense of it. The brutality of it." For Stanley, in particular, time stopped.

The immediate aftermath was "horrendous", Maggie said. Their lives had been turned upside down. Maggie was grieving for her close friend, Barbara, and conscious, at the same time, of the suffering Stanley was going through. And then there were four young boys. Stanley was trying to watch out and care for his two nephews and be a father. But his own two boys were grieving: they loved their Uncle Herbie and were close to their two cousins.

Maggie said, "we learned to live with it." Barbara went back to work in the business that her sister had in Armagh. The families continued to support and help each other with child-care. They practically lived together. Maggie said, "They blended together." Stanley and Herbie's family helped by creating fun times for the four boys, sleep overs and arranging days of games and activities.

The Fears...

"First of all, I feared that everyone belonging to me would die. The reality that the terrorists might return for their intended target never left me as a fear. I feared for my children that they would become bitter and we both actively sought to dissuade negative thinking or bitterness within a divided community. Stanley's reaction was to pour himself fully into the fight against terrorism through his work with the UDR. This also made me fearful for his health and safety."

Faith in the Lord Jesus Christ...

"My minister, Rev Bachelor, was very good to us and supportive in bringing comfort from scripture. However, as unbelievers, where we appreciated his input, it was not necessarily impacting our grief as non-practicing Christians.

I had a Christian milkman who began to talk to me about Herbie's death and the reality of eternity and the need to be prepared for heaven. He gave me a 'salvation' New Testament, which I began to read. Through reading the Scriptures and conviction of sin and a need to prepare for heaven, I became a born again Christian one year later. My sister Violet was a born-again believer and I asked her how to get saved. I attended a local gospel meeting with her and her husband and gave my life to the Lord on March 13th, 1984 – one year and 10 days after Herbie's untimely death."

This Christian milkman is to be honoured for his obedience in sharing the Gospel of the Lord Jesus Christ. Maggie was very honest in saying that she "could see him far enough" on occasions. She dreaded going to the door when he called at times. But he persisted. In the week prior to Maggie's conversion, the milkman had invited her to a mission and said that he would call for her. She said "okay" but, in reality had no intention of going. When he did call, Maggie gave some lame excuse and that was the start of the Lord convicting her. "I was feeling guilty. I had become a liar." The following days were hard and Maggie didn't understand exactly what was happening in her heart. "What is wrong with me?", she questioned.

Maggie knew the Gospel and had been to many children meetings in her young years. "I must have asked Jesus into my heart a thousand times," she remembered. At the end of this difficult week, she went to a Gospel meeting. "The preacher was a Scottish evangelist and I cannot remember what he preached, but I was feeling so convicted." On making a profession of faith in the Lord Jesus, Maggie said, "I felt such relief. I had never felt such relief in my life." She went home and told Stanley what she had done, "I got saved tonight."

Maggie continued to attend the Church of Ireland, but also started to attend the Milford Christian Fellowship[107], where she was saved. She threw herself into the life of her local C.O.I. church. This was the church that Stanley and Maggie had already been attending. The Rev. John Batchelor was the minister and he supported the family in the aftermath of the murder of Herbie. In time Maggie became a member of the select vestry; she taught in the Sunday School and ran "keep fit classes" in the church. Maggie was growing in her relationship with the Lord Jesus. She challenged the practice of confirmation in the C.O.I. because she felt it was just "going through the motions" regarding faith. Rev. Batchelor was not opposed and, in fact, encouraged her to share and preach the Gospel as she prepared individuals for confirmation. Maggie said, "people need a relationship with Jesus."

In these early days you can trace the Lord working in Maggie's life and giving her a desire to know Him in a more personal way. A passion for God's word grew as she used Spurgeon's morning and evenings Bible readings. The experiences of Old Testament saints encouraged her to expect the same for herself: "Enoch walked with God. I can walk with God"; "God spoke directly to them. He can speak directly to me"; "Solomon had a compassionate heart. I can have a compassionate heart". Maggie was searching and wanting to have a

---

107 This church was a Brethren Assembly

reality of experience with the Lord; "I was not a Bible woman before my conversion. I wanted to be real with God."

The first time Maggie heard the Lord speaking to her from the Bible, was when she was reading Genesis 50:20: *"You intended to harm me, but God intended it for good to accomplish what is now being done, the saving of many lives."* As time went on, this first experience of hearing the voice of God began to bear fruit in her life.

Because of some health issues, Maggie left nursing and went to train as a social worker in the community. On finishing the training, a Bible passage started to repeat itself in her heart, *"Go through, go through the gates."* Isaiah 62:10 (KJV). At this time Maggie developed some further health issues and a job opportunity arose in the community. However, this expression was still playing in her mind: "Go through the gates." She wanted to know God's will for her life. She considered herself hopeless at interviews and, in view of the current health problems, she kept thinking of backing out of the interview. But this expression kept bombarding her heart, "Go through the gates." She also searched her heart regarding motives for applying for such a job; "there was a social standing with the job."

"I didn't pull the plug on the interview and on the morning of the interview I received news that my health scare was negative." Maggie went for the interview; was successful and went on to work with deaf people in the community. As one of her heroes, Enoch, "walked with God", so Maggie was growing in her walk with the Lord and learning to depend on Gods' word.

There have been many personal challenges for Maggie. A number of friends and family members died early in their lives from cancer or faced other heart-breaking circumstances. Much sadness came in a relatively short period of time in her life. Maggie had asked the

Lord for a compassionate heart. "To become compassionate, I went through some tough circumstances."

While working as a social worker in the community, a colleague mentioned how she would like to increase her counselling skills. Maggie liked the idea and went with her colleague and achieved an advanced diploma in counselling. She is very honest about this: "There was nothing spiritual about this." She had not sought God about this but decided to go along to develop further her own counselling skills.

Shortly after receiving her diploma a door opened for Maggie to be involved in Christian ministry. A Christian ministry called, "Foundation Ministries"[108] happened to be visiting Maggie's local church one evening. They were there to celebrate twenty-five years of Christian service. The leader of the ministry was Jimmy Evans and Maggie knew Jimmy from the times he had come to preach in the church. After the service, she approached him and offered her help in any way. She was invited to join the ministry's executive committee. This group met every month. Before any discussion, each meeting started with prayer and a member sharing something from God's word. Eventually Maggie was asked to bring one of these devotionals. God was already challenging her with the story of Jacob and his wrestling with the Lord. An expression gripped her heart: "Are we going to persist for the blessing or are we going to resist the blessing?" Maggie shared this challenge and a set of discussions was triggered that resulted in a change of leadership at Foundation Ministries.

The leader at the time expressed her heart by saying that she felt God was leading her to another ministry. This executive group spent time in prayer and fasting for a way forward. The Lord was speaking personally to Maggie through Scriptures in Joshua, Nehemiah and

---

[108] "Foundation Ministries" was established by the Rev. David Greer. He felt that there were Christians who were unable to talk to their own ministers about some life issues and faith. The service, which was free, was for such people

Ruth. During a subsequent meeting, a member of the group shared what God had put on his heart, using the very scriptures that God had personally given to Maggie. She had them all written down on paper and was taken aback as Scriptures the Lord had given to her were spoken out by other members of the group. A key Bible passage was: *"Moses my servant is dead…"*.

Maggie relates how, during these discussions, her "knees were knocking and her legs felt like jelly" as the group discussed a way forward with a likely change of leadership for the ministry. The group asked the question, "Is there a Joshua here?" and one member shared that the Lord wanted the ministry *"to go in and take possession of the land."* Joshua 1:11. Maggie had the same promise written down again. At this point, Maggie stepped forward and said, "I believe God is calling me" and she became the director in December 2011.

God had a new chapter to write in the story of Foundation Ministries and Maggie was to be part of it. The Lord had been preparing her for this moment. In the years following her conversion, the Lord had developed her love for His word and she had proved that God's word could be depended upon. The Lord had formed a passionate and caring heart in her and she knew what the voice of God sounded like. Through God's sovereignty, Maggie had gone on a course to develop her counselling skills and she received an accredited diploma.

Through the many difficult times, Maggie had proved the truth of Jesus' words: *"Very truly I tell you, unless a kernel of wheat falls to the ground and dies, it remains only a single seed. But if it dies, it produces many seeds."* John 12:24. After coming to faith in the Lord Jesus, she saw continuing sorrow unfold in the family. Her sorrow was a death experience. Suffering can either take us away from God or drive us toward the Lord. Maggie followed the latter path and only the Lord knows the tears she shed before the Lord for her own life and for the Burrows family.

The work of Foundation Ministries has increased and today there are eight skilled workers within the ministry. Their website gives this insight:

"Foundation Ministries is based in Co. Armagh Northern Ireland. We offer accessible and comprehensive Biblical counselling to those on a journey of restoration, healing and wholeness in Christ.

Established 1979, we are an interdenominational ministry of counselling, evangelism and training, managed by a committee made up of born-again Christians from various denominations. We are a registered charity, supported solely by donations to the work."

Since becoming the director of Foundation Ministries, Maggie, and the team that God brought around her, have experienced clear direction and provision from the Lord. Through contacts in Athlone, the ministry adopted a "Biblical counselling" programme. She said, "This has brought such freedom into the counselling process. God comes into the room."

Another area where the ministry experienced the provision of God was in regard to premises. The ministry had offices but they were four floors up and it became evident that they needed a ground floor building. Again, through hearing God's voice through His word and then appearing on a BBC series called "City of Faith"[109], God brought across their path a Christian man who offered them "a blank cheque". In less than a year, through the help of local tradesmen and volunteers, Foundation Ministries had new ground floor premises and the Lord's blessing and favour has continued to increase on the ministry.

---

109 "City of Faith" was a BBC series telling the stories of faith of people who lived in and around Armagh. Armagh has been the ecclesiastical capital of Ireland since the fifth century, when St Patrick founded his church there.

"You intended to harm me, but God intended it for good to accomplish what is now being done, the saving of many lives." Genesis 50:20

This is the Bible verse which heads up this chapter on Maggie Burrows, because it is the first Bible verse that the Lord spoke into Maggie's life following her conversion. "I wasn't a Bible woman but Genesis 50:20 was the first time I heard God's voice." Undoubtedly God has fulfilled this promise in Maggie's life and she is bearing much fruit.

March 3rd, 1984, was a very bleak day for Maggie and the Burrows family. She was not born-again. She was religious, but had no relationship with the Lord Jesus Christ. Thank God for an obedient milkman who pursued her with the challenge of the Gospel. Thank God He was pursuing Maggie because He had a purpose for her life.

"You intended to harm me, but God intended it for good to accomplish what is now being done, the saving of many lives."

The years of the Troubles in Northern Ireland were a vile expression of evil and wickedness. What was intended? Families living with bitterness, individuals seeking revenge and the break-up of community? But, with God, things can be turned around. Eternity will reveal the many, many lives that have been touched by God's love through Maggie and the team at Foundation Ministries. Joseph was used to save his own family and the nation of Egypt. Maggie and her team have been used, and continue to be used by God, in the hurting and grief-stricken communities of Armagh. To Him be the glory and the praise.

The Story Of David Clements

"Precious in the sight of the LORD is the death of His godly ones."
Psalm 116:15 (NASB)

David Clement's father was Constable William (Billy) Clements and he was murdered on December 7th, 1985, by the East Tyrone Brigade of the Provisional IRA. He was on duty at Ballygawley police station. David writes, "As he went out to his car, to go home for his evening meal, there was a ring at the station gate. As he answered it, shooting broke out, he was shot in the face and then again in the head as he lay on the ground. Another colleague was also murdered before a bomb was left which destroyed the station. The others in the station had a miraculous escape."[110] The police station was destroyed. Homes in the vicinity were wrecked and the local community were in shock. The explosion cut off electricity supplies and the whole area was in darkness. The telephone system was also disrupted."

The colleague who was murdered was Constable George Gilliland. The personal cost of this attack was that two wives were widowed, eight children lost their fathers, and two families were devastated and deeply hurt.

That day Billy had changed shifts with a friend, to enable him to attend a wedding. David noticed that his father was always willing

---

110 Spencer G. "Forgiving and Remembering in Northern Ireland" (2011) London, Continuum International Publishing Group.

to swap shifts with colleagues but that he would never ask anyone to swap shifts for him.

What was the motive for the attack? There was an IRA campaign at the time to blow up police stations and then ensure that they were never rebuilt. This included threats not only to police officers, but to construction workers at RUC sites. Therefore, David believes the motive for shooting his father "had more to do with his bottle green uniform than the fact that he was a Protestant."

Who was Billy Clements?

Billy was born on June 3rd, 1933, and was converted in 1953, particularly influenced by his involvement with the Boys Brigade in Shankill Road Methodist Church. He made his commitment to Christ at the family home in the Shankill area of Belfast. David writes: "His faith grew over the years and part of his regular spiritual discipline was to read his Bible every day."

Billy was married to Ella and they had five children. The family had spent some time living in South Africa, where Billy worked in the shoe trade. In 1969 the family (husband, wife and four children) came back to Northern Ireland for a holiday. In the spring of 1970, the family returned to live permanently in Northern Ireland. Initially they lived with a grandfather, who had been recently widowed, until a new house was built in Ballygawley, County Tyrone. Billy's widow still lives in that home.

On Billy's return to Northern Ireland, he worked as managing director for McAfee's, a shoe business in Belfast. Because of bomb attacks in the city, David remembers the message appearing at times on the news, "Would all keyholders return" and so his father, whatever hour of the day, would drive from Ballgawley to Belfast, a journey of over

50 miles each way, to check on the company's premises. Later in the 1970's, Billy left McAfees and went to work for a smaller business near the family home in Ballygawley. To help the family finances, he started to serve as a part-time reservist in the RUC. In time this resulted in him taking up a full-time position with the RUC.

Billy was on duty when he was murdered by the Provisional IRA on Saturday 7th December 1985. The headline the following week in the local paper, The Tyrone Courier, read,

"TWO DEAD IN HORROR ATTACK ON POLICE STATION."

In the article detailing the murders, there was this story about Billy Clements: "A local councillor, Mr Sammy Brush, mentioned how William Clements had helped him on one occasion: 'I was delivering mail near Ballygawley when I was ambushed and shot by the IRA. It was due to the help and speed at which Willie Clements took me to hospital that my life was saved.'"[111]

At Billy's funeral, the Rev. Skillen[112] gave this insight into his life: "Bill Clements and his wife Ella and family had paid Ulster a rare tribute. In 1969[113], when the troubles were starting many people decided to emigrate. Bill and Ella, however, decided to come back from South Africa and 'share our troubled life'. And they did so believing that was God's will for their lives."

When the family had moved to South Africa, Billy was already a local preacher with the Methodist Church. He continued in this calling after the move from Northern Ireland and, Rev. Skillen continued,

---

111 Tyrone Courier Wednesday 11th December 1985.
112 Rev. Hamilton Skillen was the President of the Methodist Church in Ireland at the time of William Clements' murder.
113 The family actually returned in spring 1970.

"He preached with great effectiveness to both blacks and whites... One of the great influences in his life was the Renewal Movement.[114] From the time he discovered the power of the Holy Spirit he found the power of Love. That love transcended all barriers of nationality and creed and social standing. He became a man of remarkable talent for getting alongside all kinds of people, that was quite unique. His spiritual exuberance drew people to him and he in turn pointed them to Christ."

On his return to Northern Ireland Billy became a director of the Lay Methodist Movement and played a leading role in taking teams on mission to Methodist churches throughout Britain and Ireland.

Rev. Skillen paid this tribute: "As a result many congregations were stimulated into new life because of those visits. Bill Clements's exuberance and joyful nature was magnetic. As Methodism was enriched by his life it is now impoverished by his death."

A few days after the funeral a senior police detective visited the family home. Billy's gun could not be accounted for at the police station. The house was searched but it could not be found. The only remaining possibility was that the person who had killed his father had taken the gun as the gang escaped. The family faced this dreadful situation: the gun would be used to kill other innocent lives. David said, "This was almost too painful to comprehend."

The Bible Reading for the Day...

On the December 7th, 1985, Billy left home to go to work, with his Bible open at Psalm 10. David writes, "It was probably the last

---

[114] The Renewal Movement can be dated from the 1960's. It was a movement throughout the Christian church. The particular emphasis was the person and work and presence of the Holy Spirit.

portion of Scripture that he read before he went to be with his Lord later that day."

Psalm 10

"Why, LORD, do you stand far off?
  Why do you hide yourself in times of trouble?
In his arrogance the wicked man hunts down the weak,
  who are caught in the schemes he devises.
He boasts about the cravings of his heart;
  he blesses the greedy and reviles the LORD.
In his pride the wicked man does not seek him;
  in all his thoughts there is no room for God.
His ways are always prosperous;
  your laws are rejected by him;
  he sneers at all his enemies.
He says to himself, 'Nothing will ever shake me.'
  He swears, 'No one will ever do me harm.'
His mouth is full of lies and threats;
  trouble and evil are under his tongue.
He lies in wait near the villages;
  from ambush he murders the innocent.
His eyes watch in secret for his victims;
  like a lion in cover he lies in wait.
He lies in wait to catch the helpless;
  he catches the helpless and drags them off in his net.
His victims are crushed, they collapse;
  they fall under his strength.
He says to himself, 'God will never notice;
  he covers his face and never sees.'
Arise, LORD! Lift up your hand, O God.
  Do not forget the helpless.

Why does the wicked man revile God?
　　Why does he say to himself,
　　'He won't call me to account'?
But you, God, see the trouble of the afflicted;
　　you consider their grief and take it in hand.
The victims commit themselves to you;
　　you are the helper of the fatherless.
Break the arm of the wicked man;
　　call the evildoer to account for his wickedness
　　that would not otherwise be found out.
The L*ORD* *is King for ever and ever;*
　　the nations will perish from his land.
You, L*ORD,* *hear the desire of the afflicted;*
　　you encourage them, and you listen to their cry,
defending the fatherless and the oppressed,
　　so that mere earthly mortals
　　will never again strike terror."

This is one of the psalms of lament. Someone has given this description of lament:

"To lament is to mourn before the Lord over all the things that are not right in the world, to be honest about the pain they bring…yet to thrust our hope on His ultimate promise that one day, He will make things right."[115] What was Billy Clements speaking to the Lord about that morning? What pains were in his heart about the situation in Northern Ireland?

Some feel that we have lost the Biblical skill of lamenting before the Lord. I found this comment in the book "Considering Grace", which is centred around experiences that Christian people suffered through the Troubles: "The stories in this book suggest that one

---

115 See "FindingtheLife.com – A Unique Song".

way we might begin to remember in the present is to recognise our shared suffering and to respond to it with lament. Lament has been defined as a passionate expression of grief or sorrow. It is a common practice in the Hebrew Bible, including the book of Lamentations and the Psalms."[116]

On the morning of December 7th, Billy Clements was reading a psalm of lament: "Why, LORD, do you stand far off? Why do you hide yourself in times of trouble?" In previous weeks there had been a number of murders: the IRA had shot a Catholic civilian and a Catholic UDR man; they had also planted a bomb and a landmine which accounted for two more deaths and the UDA/UFF[117] had murdered a Catholic civilian in the weeks prior to the attack on Ballygawley police station.

Perhaps Billy had these horrific murders on his mind as he sought the Lord about the situation in Northern Ireland. Although 1985 saw the lowest number of murders in Northern Ireland since 1970, there was unrest over the political discussions that were taking place to establish the Anglo-Irish Agreement. Loyalist paramilitaries were attacking police homes across the country. The Unionist politicians were angry about the discussions between Dublin and London and felt excluded from the proposals being discussed. There were riots in the loyalist town of Portadown and the "Protestant police force faced the unionist accusation that they had betrayed their community by quelling anti-Agreement protest."[118]

---

116 Ganiel G. and Yohanis J. (2019) "Considering Grace: Presbyterians and the Troubles". Ireland, Merrion Press.

117 The Ulster Freedom Fighters (UFF) were a group within the UDA who were tasked with paramilitary attacks. This was a cover name, so that the UDA would not be outlawed. The British government outlawed the UFF in November 1973, but the UDA itself was not proscribed as a terrorist group until August 1992. (Wikipedia).

118 McKittrick D., Feeney B., Thornton C. and Kelters S. (1999) "Lost Lives. The stories of the men, women and children who died as a result of the Northern Ireland Troubles", Edinburgh, Mainstream Publishing Company Ltd.

In the early part of 1985, the worst attack on the police service took place. The IRA launched a mortar attack on Newry police station on February 28th, and nine police officers were killed; seven policemen and two policewomen. Three children lost their father. RUC Chief Constable Sir John Hermon[119], wrote this about the attack: "Photographs of the nine dead officers later appeared in the Police Review, and looking at their faces, pictured together on one page, disturbed me greatly. Nevertheless, I kept the magazine open in a drawer of my office desk until the day I retired and cleared out the office. It still lies open at the same page in my study at home."[120] Billy, no doubt as part of the RUC, would have felt the sadness of this atrocity very deeply. They were colleagues.

In front of Billy that morning of December 7th, was this prayer from Psalm 10: *"Arise, Lord! Lift up your hand, O God. Do not forget the helpless. Why does the wicked man revile God? Why does he say to himself, 'He won't call me to account'? But you, God, see the trouble of the afflicted; you consider their grief and take it in hand. The victims commit themselves to you; you are the helper of the fatherless."* The five murders in weeks before December 7th, left 13 children without a father. Two of the murders were of single men. The mother of one said, "This morning I had 6 sons. Now I have only 5."

Billy's wife, Ella, said this on the death of her husband: "He saw himself as a policeman for all people, not just for the Protestants or the Catholics. He thought that as a Christian he could bring people together through Christ." I do think that Billy's involvement with the Renewal Movement and his heart for the Catholic community would have enlarged both the breadth and depth of his intercession for the people of Northern Ireland and beyond. The striking thought is this:

---

[119] Sir John Hermon OBE QPM (23 November 1928 – 6 November 2008) was the Chief Constable of the Royal Ulster Constabulary from 1980–1989. (Wikipedia).

[120] McKittrick D., Feeney B., Thornton C. and Kelters S. (1999) "Lost Lives. The stories of the men, women and children who died as a result of the Northern Ireland Troubles", Edinburgh, Mainstream Publishing Company Ltd.

in the morning William was talking to his Lord, by the early evening he was in His presence.

Some twenty years later, on September 11, 2005, David preached on Psalm 10 for a service on Raidio Teilifis Eireann (RTE).[121] He mentioned the poignancy of verses 8-11 in regard to what happened to his father:

> *"He lies in wait near the villages; from ambush he murders the innocent. His eyes watch in secret for his victims; like a lion in cover, he lies in wait. He lies in wait to catch the helpless; he catches the helpless and drags them off in his net. His victims are crushed, they collapse; they fall under his strength. He says to himself, 'God will never notice; he covers his face and never sees.'"*

The Tyrone Courier gave this account of the incident in December 1985[122]: "The two men who died were 34-year-old Constable George Gilliland of Clabby Road, Fivemiletown and 52-year-old Billy Clements of Crewe Road, Ballygawley. They were both shot dead in a hail of bullets by gunmen who had taken up positions behind a wall opposite the Police Station. It is understood one of the constables had gone to the gate to let his colleague out when the terrorists struck in cold blooded fashion killing both men instantly."

David closed the sermon with this thought on verse 13: "Why does the wicked man revile God? Why does he say to himself, 'He won't call me to account'? The wicked man is wrong. He is very wrong. God WILL call him to account. It may not be today, it may not be tomorrow, but one day God will call him to account. On the one hand we should feel glad about that. We all like to think that in the

---

121 RTE is the national broadcaster of Ireland headquartered in Donnybrook, Dublin. It both produces and broadcasts programmes on television, radio and online.(Wikipedia). It was a service remembering the 9/11 attack in New York.
122 Tyrone Courier Wednesday 11h December 1985.

end justice will be done and that people like Hitler will not get away with their terrible crimes. On the other hand, it is also a profoundly discomforting thought – I may not be a mass murderer, but I will be held accountable by God for all my little grubby sins. How foolish it would be to have no room in my thoughts for God; to think that God has not noticed my sins, or forgotten them; or to say that there is not going to be a judgement day."

Where was David?

"It was a cold clear night in early December 1985. I had just enjoyed a Christmas party with the youth group from the church I was attending in Belfast. Attempts to contact me earlier had failed and I arrived at my house to find the door open. An old flatmate and close friend, who still had a key, was waiting for me with the minister from the church. The seven words of conversation that followed are still vivid in my mind. 'David, your dad's been shot', 'Dead?', 'Yes.' It may seem a brutal way to have conveyed such news, but best friends do know best.

As I had been going out for the evening in Belfast, my dad was about to go home from the police station in Ballygawley. As he went out to his car, there was a ring at the station gate. As he answered it, shooting broke out. He was shot in the face and then again in the head as he lay on the ground. Another colleague was murdered before a bomb was left which destroyed the station. The others in the station had a miraculous escape.

I travelled the 50 miles home with my friend and his wife (a cousin of mine) in silence. What could any of us have said? The first person to greet me as I arrived home was my mother. She came outside into the cold darkness and embraced me and said, 'Isn't it terrible'. I felt for the first time the real pain of the 'Troubles'. After all these years it is still painful to recount this story."[123]

For me, the cold-heartedness and the calculating nature of this attack is demonstrated by a terrorist, going up to Billy, who was lying on the ground helpless and bleeding, and shooting him in the head at point-blank range.

What about Mrs Clements?

This was a dreadful experience for the family. David says, "I had always known that my mother was a remarkable woman, but her conduct in the days that followed added proof beyond doubt. My mother showed remarkable grace. In my view it was of supernatural origin. Over a few days I guess that about 500 people called at our home and my mother spoke a word of grace to virtually every one of them – everyone from the local parish priest to the Rev. Ian Paisley. Perhaps most notable she welcomed the visit of some members of a neighbouring family with very strong republican sympathies who may well have applauded the 'daring raid' which left my father lying dead on the ground.

A day or two after my father was killed, my mother and I did an interview with one of the local television stations. I can't remember all that we said and I can't remember exactly what was later broadcast, but I do remember this. We commented on my father's faith, a faith that we shared. We did not speak at that stage of forgiveness but we did speak without bitterness and pleaded for no retaliations. On a number of occasions in the years that followed I was made aware that

---

[123] Spencer G. "Forgiving and Remembering in Northern Ireland" (2011) London, Continuum International Publishing Group.

those comments did have a particular and positive influence on some who might otherwise have responded differently."[124]

How did David respond?

Because, following Billy's murder, his gun could not be found either at the police station or at the family home the fear was that it would be used to murder others. David said, "That thought did add passion" to the prayers that he made to his Lord.

He explains further, "One thing that I did was to pray for the men who had killed him in cold blood. I prayed two things for them, and as far as I know my own heart, I was sincere in both requests – and in the order in which I prayed them.

First, I prayed that they would repent of the evil they had done, that they would give up their horrible violence and that they would be transformed by the love of Jesus Christ and then we would be brothers and, by the grace of God, I would certainly be enabled to forgive them.

The second prayer was this. If they would not repent and their hearts were hardened beyond redemption, I prayed that God would judge them in this life and that they would be prevented from inflicting similar sufferings on other families like mine. It gives me no pleasure to say that I believe that the second of those prayers was the one that was answered, though the final day of judgement is yet to be.

About 18 months later, while I was working as an assistant pastor in Enniskillen, I was travelling home to my flat quite late at night. On

---

[124] Spencer G. "Forgiving and Remembering in Northern Ireland" (2011) London, Continuum International Publishing Group.

the car radio there was a news bulletin which reported an attack on the Police station in Loughgall[125]. It was a very similar type of attack to the one on Ballygawley station in which my father was killed.

This time it seemed that the security forces had advance warning of the attack and this time it was the IRA unit that came under surprise attack. Eight of them were killed. As I drove and listened to this news report, I had a strange feeling that I find hard to explain. I was just a few hundred yards from my flat; I parked the car and sat in silence for some time. I sensed that something was over. It was as if a quiet voice said to me – the men you were praying for are now dead. The following day a seal of confirmation was given to me when I was told that my father's gun had been recovered at the scene in Loughgall."[126]

The sad thing was this: until its recovery, the gun had been used to murder three people, one of whom was a member of the UDR.

A Servant of the Lord Jesus Christ…

David went to Queens University in 1979 to study medicine. He had become a Christian during a Beach Mission in County Sligo in 1974. In the years following he became involved in Christian groups both in school and at university. In David's first year at university, he experienced the loss of a friend, John Donaldson, who was shot by the IRA. John was seen coming out of a police station and the IRA thought he was a member of the security services. In fact, he was a trainee solicitor delivering paperwork to the police station.

---

125 The Loughgall ambush took place on 8th May 1987 in the village of Loughgall, County Armagh, Northern Ireland. An eight-man unit of the Provisional Irish Republican Army (IRA) launched an attack on the Royal Ulster Constabulary (RUC) base in the village.(Wikipedia).

126 Spencer G. "Forgiving and Remembering in Northern Ireland" (2011) London, Continuum International Publishing Group.

In 1984, David was involved in a series of Christian mission events at Queens called "The Missing Peace". One of the events involved a panel of people who had been directly affected by the Troubles, including a policeman's widow and three ex-paramilitaries, from the IRA, the INLA and the UVF, all of whom had been converted to Christ during their time in prison." David recalls this as a very striking event: "The place was packed and very tense as each panel member shared their testimonies." It was around this time that David sensed a call to Christian ministry. He qualified as a doctor but in 1986 "I re-heard the call of God to serve Him in the Methodist ministry. That call has taken me to Enniskillen, Warrenpoint, Woodvale/Shankill and then Belvoir."[127]

It was during David's ministry at Woodvale/Shankill in Belfast that he had his first encounter with terrorism as a minister. The Shankill Road bombing was carried out by the IRA on October 23rd, 1993, and is one of the most notorious incidents of the Troubles in Northern Ireland. Ten people were killed: one of the IRA bombers, a UDA member and eight Protestant civilians, two of whom were children. More than 50 people were wounded.[128]

David went to the scene and was able to comfort a family that lost a wife and a father-in-law. The casualties were taken to the Mater Hospital. David took the husband and the wife to the hospital and was with them when they were told that their two loved ones were dead. He explains, "My own personal experience gave me the resource to help."

---

[127] Spencer G. "Forgiving and Remembering in Northern Ireland" (2011) London, Continuum International Publishing Group.

[128] The IRA aimed to assassinate the leadership of the Loyalist Ulster Defence Association (UDA), supposedly attending a meeting above Frizzell's fish shop on the Shankill Road, Belfast. Two IRA members disguised as deliverymen entered the shop carrying a bomb, which detonated prematurely. (Wikipedia).

The next step for David was to be involved with WAVE – Widows Against Violence Empower. This group was established to help and support people traumatised, bereaved and injured by the Troubles. David was invited to be part of the management committee and is still part of the service. Through WAVE and also through his own pastoral work, David has been involved directly with many families affected by the violence of the Troubles. He has found that he has been able to use his experience with pain to help others.

This reaching out has known no boundaries. During his time in Woodvale, he started to attend Catholic funerals which resulted from the Troubles. He was able to feel and empathise because of his own experience and bring a witness to the Lord God into the situation.

David is very honest about the negative feelings that still well up at times when memories come flooding back regarding his father and there are still times when, understandably, he struggles with his emotions. He recalls a recent experience at the 25th anniversary of the killing of two RUC community police officers. The son of one of the officers was only six years old at the time. He is now 31 years old and, looking at his own children, he reflected, "I understand what loss is." David said, "That made me weep." Over the years, he has watched his mother attend family events as a widow. When David's first baby was born, he took the newborn to his father's grave to introduce the child. David commented, "He would have been a great grandfather."

Since the murder of his father, David has received many invitations from the media to speak about his story. In recent months, he has contributed to a debate in Parliament regarding the legacy of the Troubles.

David is very clear about the difficulties that are faced regarding forgiveness and justice: "In Northern Ireland there is little chance that many victims will ever receive an apology. Their beloved husband or son, father or brother was seen in the eyes of others as a legitimate target, hence no crime was committed and talk of apology inappropriate. The best we can hope for, it seems, is an expression of regret for the hurt caused on all sides. There is a great danger here for the victims. With no prospect of meaningful repentance, there is the possibility that the victim will be trapped in a bitter spirit. But it need not be so."[129]

He is also very clear about a way forward: "Whether or not the perpetrator acknowledges his guilt, the victim, in response to insult or injury, may choose to take the initiative and develop, by the grace of God, a forgiving spirit... A forgiving spirit is better than a bitter spirit."[130]

Developing such a spirit will not only be of great benefit to the victim, but also a benefit to the guilty and a benefit to society as a whole in Northern Ireland. David has written and spoken about what a forgiving spirit looks like and what attitudes and behaviours it requires. He would be the first to say that such a spirit doesn't come overnight but, he would also say, "Start by making the decision to choose to be forgiving". For a Christian we have a tremendous example in the person of the Lord Jesus Christ and the forgiveness we have received from God through faith.

There is one final story to include from David's ministry. Following the bomb attack on Frizzell's fish shop on the Shankill Road, Belfast , which was mentioned earlier, there were retaliations from the loyalist paramilitaries. David went to visit one of the families in West Belfast that suffered as a consequence. He was wearing his clerical collar and was received politely in the home. At some point, David was able to

---

[129] Spencer G. "Forgiving and Remembering in Northern Ireland" (2011) London, Continuum International Publishing Group.

[130] Spencer G. "Forgiving and Remembering in Northern Ireland" (2011) London, Continuum International Publishing Group.

share, "I have some idea of the things you are going through because my dad was killed at work." The atmosphere in the room changed: "The whole room came again to shake hands with me and were saying, 'This guy knows what we are going through'." There have been many other occasions where David's own experience of the Troubles has given him opportunity to bring a deeply personal Christian pastoral ministry into the situation.

David was 25 years old when his father was killed. When asked what qualities he had seen in his father which had influenced his own life, David mentioned his father's commitment to the family; his devotion to his wife, his enjoyment of holidays and sports with the family and his willingness to leave work in Belfast and to take a significant reduction in wages to work nearer to home and family. Most significant of all was his father's Christian faith.

David had travelled with his father to hear him preach at different meetings, sometimes across the border in the Republic of Ireland. He saw how important God's word was to his father and that legacy continues through David. Billy is dead but his Christian witness lives on through his son and only eternity will reveal the blessing David has been to many people in their sufferings as a result of his experiences throughout the Troubles.

> *"Precious in the sight of the LORD is the death of His godly ones."*
> Psalm 116:15 (NASB)

This was the verse of scripture that the Lord brought before David in the hours after the murder of his father. Within a few days, David's mother also came across this same scripture. David said, "She didn't know that there was such a verse in the Bible." It is a verse which brought consolation to the family and gave assurance that Billy Clements was with the Lord Jesus in Heaven.

For the terrorist group that attacked Ballygawley police station and murdered two officers on December 7th, 1985, it was just a legitimate target in their murderous campaign against the law enforcement agencies of Great Britain. Their callousness in shooting Billy Clements in the head, after he had already been shot and was lying helpless on the floor, was just wicked, but in God's eyes, the murder of Billy Clements was precious.

One Bible commentator writes, "...the death of God's loyal subjects is too costly for him to treat lightly."[131] The Lord values those who love Him. The Lord values those whom He loves. On December 7th, 1985, although Billy Clements body was lying mortally injured on the ground, Billy wasn't there because he had been taken into the presence of God in Heaven. He had entered into the fullness of his salvation in the Lord Jesus.

---

131 Eveson P. "Psalms" (2015) Welwyn Garden City, EP Books.

More Stories Of Faith

Derek Kidd...

"My name is Chris. Throughout the Troubles I served as a part time fire officer, attending many incidents in the line of duty. Often the danger was all too evident, and by the grace of God, I was uninjured.

But the day that really hit home, as far as the Troubles are concerned, was the day my brother, Derek was murdered. A part time UDR soldier, he was ambushed when he was unarmed. However, the moment didn't stop there. Sickeningly, in the period up to his funeral, our family received sinister anonymous phone calls.

But, during this time, the ministry of our church, Christ Church Strabane, and especially the Rector, Canon Ernest Lovell, was an enormous help. Many of my fellow parishioners joined together in a packed church for Derek's funeral. Again, the church was packed for the Memorial Service. Even many Roman Catholics expressed their sympathy and support, although unable to attend due to the threat to their own lives. All of this helped keep our family strong during a very turbulent time.

Our Christian faith enabled us to be of help to other victims of terrorist violence. When one such victim was attacked in retaliation for Derek's murder, Dean Good and myself, with the help of Canon

Lovell, went to visit the victim's family in the notorious Bogside area of Londonderry.

What can I say about the experience? Simply, you'll never forget, but you do learn to live with it. Above all, my Christian faith helped me not only to cope with what happened, and was happening almost on a daily basis, but to rise above it and see a greater purpose, a higher Power, at work in my life."

Derek Kidd was killed on November 18th, 1976, in Londonderry. He was 37 years old, and married with three children. "The UDR corporal from Glen Road, Strabane, was shot at point-blank range by two republican gunmen in the Waterside area of the city as he was leaving a hut on a Housing Executive building site on Trench Road. Two youths carried out the attack at around 2.30pm. A Catholic man, John Toland, was killed by the UFF in retaliation on November 22nd, 1976, and the IRA responded by killing Joseph Glover. Corporal Kidd's wife issued a statement pleading for no retaliation for her husband's death and dissociated herself from a claim by the UFF that they shot John Toland in revenge. Corporal Kidd was buried at Leckpatrick Parish Church after a service at Christ Church, Strabane. In September 1976, the Church of Ireland Bishop of Derry and Raphoe dedicated a silver chalice in memory of the victim at Christ Church."[132]

Joseph Wilson...

Joseph was murdered by an IRA gunman on October 26th, 1976.

---

[132] McKittrick D., Feeney B., Thornton C. and Kelters S. (1999) "Lost Lives. The stories of the men, women and children who died as a result of the Northern Ireland Troubles", Edinburgh, Mainstream Publishing Company Ltd.

He was 53 years old, married to Anna and they had nine children: four boys and five girls with ages ranging from 8 to 28 (four of the family were married). His life was taken up with his home, his work, the UDR, and his church.

Maggie Burrows[133], whose story is told in chapter 6, said this in regard to Joseph:

"Joseph was a loyal Christian man. He was a born-again man. He was a very, very upright Christian man."

"The time was 11.15am, and in broad daylight, the killer calmly awaited his opportunity to go after his prey and gun Mr Wilson to death. Obviously, he waited until Lester's Supermarket at English Street, where Mr Wilson was busy behind the bacon counter, had emptied of customers.

Perhaps he paced up and down the pavement. Or perhaps his luck was in immediately, and the shop was empty. Anyway, it was a slack time of day. Then, the killer walked casually between the high display shelves and arrived at the bacon department where Mr Wilson was manager. Police believe that the killer even pointed to some merchandise behind Mr Wilson, as he turned his back, the gunman then calmly pulled a pistol, from his pocket, and carefully aimed at the defenceless shop-keeper.

One, two, three bullets pierced his back, and he slumped to the floor, dying, his blood pouring on to the polished floor. Calmly, the murderer turned on his heel, and made off to where – the police

---

133 One of Joseph's daughters was called Barbara. Barbara and Maggie were best friends and they married twin brothers. Maggie married Stanley Burrows and Barbara married Herbie Burrows. Barbara was pregnant with her first born when her father was murdered. Barbara's husband, Herbie, was murdered on 3rd March 1984.

believe – a getaway car was waiting for him across the street at the head of Cathedral Road."[134]

Joseph was described as a man "who hated violence. The only way he saw was a straight, true path to law and order, and nobody – friend or terrorist – would deviate him from that path."[135] His employer described Joseph as "a great worker and a harmless man who caused nobody any offence". Joseph and his wife, Anna, lived at Lisdown, South Armagh. The family kept various animals at their seven-acre property and attended Knappagh Presbyterian Church. Although the ownership of the supermarket, where Joseph was employed, had changed hands a few times, he had in fact worked at the same premises for 35 years, from the time he was twenty.

One headline about the murder of Joseph caught my attention: "Years of ruthless intimidation end in callous killing." This intimidation was carried out by Republican terrorists.

"Over the past four years, Mr Wilson had been subjected to an assassination attempt, an armed robbery at his isolated home at Lisdown, threatening letters and phone calls, hoax bomb calls, countless incidents of shots being fired at his home.

The first of the terror incidents aimed at Mr Wilson was in September 1972, when armed and masked men forced their way into the house at Lisdown, three miles from Armagh, out the Cathedral Road. They placed the family in terror and stole his UDR uniform, as well as a shotgun. All items were consequently recovered.

This incident was followed by relentless intimidation. Phone-calls of terror were placed through to the home, threatening Mr Wilson,

---

134 Armagh Guardian 28th October 1976.
135 Armagh Guardian 28th October 1976.

and his family. On many occasions shots were fired at the home, and threatening letters were a common occurrence. And they were not idle threats, as he was to find out last year.

It was on September 11 that on returning to his parked car in the 'Shambles' yard that the gunmen first attacked him. He was lucky that time. Three bullets grazed his chest, side and back, and although he was not seriously wounded, the warning signs were clear."[136]

These two attacks saw Joseph appear in court as a witness. In regard to the shooting when he was in his car: "He subsequently gave evidence in court which helped convict a number of men."[137] Regarding the attack on the house and the family by the IRA – "he and his wife were prosecution witnesses ... A number of men were imprisoned."[138]

What about Joseph's faith?

Joseph was the Christian voice in the family. "He was a peaceable man. He was a beautiful man. He reflected his faith in his character."[139] There is something else I think we can see in this Christian man: his desire for truthfulness and justice. I think of the verse from Micah: *"He has shown you, O mortal, what is good. And what does the Lord require of you? To act justly and to love mercy and to walk humbly with your God."* Micah 6:8.

---

[136] Armagh Guardian 28th October 1976.

[137] McKittrick D., Feeney B., Thornton C. and Kelters S. (1999) "Lost Lives. The stories of the men, women and children who died as a result of the Northern Ireland Troubles", Edinburgh, Mainstream Publishing Company Ltd.

[138] McKittrick D., Feeney B., Thornton C. and Kelters S. (1999) "Lost Lives. The stories of the men, women and children who died as a result of the Northern Ireland Troubles", Edinburgh, Mainstream Publishing Company Ltd.

[139] Comments by Maggie Burrows.

Ian and Pauline Bothwell...

The Bothwell story is not about personal tragedy through the murder of a family member or friend or neighbour. It is the story of a Christian couple who were called by God to bring the Gospel into a border town in South Armagh.

This was the headline in a Northern Ireland newspaper in November 2019 -

> *"Crossfire Trust celebrates 40 years of reconciliation work on Irish border."*

"A reception has been held in a Crossmaglen Gaelic Athletic Association (GAA)[140] club for a South Armagh man and wife team who have worked for reconciliation in the area for 40 years.

Ian and Pauline Bothwell of Crossfire Trust celebrate 40 years of their work in South Armagh at Crossmaglen Rangers GAC[141] on November 9, 2019, with Newry Mourne and Down District Council Deputy Chairman Terry Andrews.

Saturday night saw a commemoration in Crossmaglen Rangers' Hall for Ian and Pauline Bothwell and volunteers from Darkley-based Crossfire Trust.

Deputy Chair of Newry Mourne and Down District Council, SDLP[142] Councillor Terry Andrews, said over 100 people attended the event.

---

[140] The Gaelic Athletic Association is Ireland's largest sporting organisation with headquarters at Croke Park, Dublin
[141] Crossmaglen Rangers Gaelic Athletic Club
[142] Social Democratic and Labour Party.

'The trust was set up with the aim of offering a listening ear, a warm bed and a cooked meal and supports those who are homeless, suffer from addiction, bereavement or mental health issues,' he said.

'It has had a significant impact on cross community relations in the area and has helped foster links between Ireland, England and the USA.'

Trust director Ian Bothwell said he would sum up the 40 years as 'an adventure with fears, thrills, disappointments and achievements.'

Originally from the border area of Tynan, Ian had just finished training as a missionary in England in 1981 and intended to go overseas until he heard BBC broadcaster David Dunseith highlighting the situation in Crossmaglen.

'I saw it was a very dangerous isolated place and the feelings of fear overwhelmed me,' he said. 'But later one of the mothers in Crossmaglen decided to trust me with their children on our summer programme. Now there are three generations of mothers attending the same programme.'

He acknowledges the area had a fearsome reputation during the Troubles. 'But the Christian response is to love your neighbour and we are sharing a gospel of peace. I am aware of ex-soldiers and their wives who have come back and have been facilitated and shown around.'

His aim for the future is to have a base in Crossmaglen 'with an old Irish kitchen where the kettle is always on'."[143]

---

143 The Newsroom, News Letter Monday 18th November 2019

Crossmaglen

Crossmaglen is a border town in County Armagh. During the Troubles the British army had a major presence in the town, along with a fortified police base. This town was a republican stronghold and a base for republican paramilitaries. The IRA had one of their South Armagh battalions in situ in Crossmaglen.[144]

During the years of conflict, Crossmaglen gained the reputation as a "gunslinging border town." The presence of British forces in the town was hated by the Catholic population and they felt harassed with this military occupation. More members of the British Army were killed in the square in Crossmaglen than in any other urban thoroughfare in Northern Ireland during the Troubles.[145]

The population of Crossmaglen saw themselves as part of Southern Ireland and had no affinity with Northern Ireland or Great Britain. There was history involved in this anti-British feeling. Crossmaglen, along with the rest of South Armagh, would have been transferred to the Irish Free State had the recommendations of the Irish Boundary Commission been enacted in 1925.[146]

It was into this town that Ian, as a single man, was called to bring the Gospel. The army and the police service brought their officers into Crossmaglen by helicopter from a military base at Bessbrook. Ian didn't have bodyguards or a bullet proof vehicle but had to make his own way into the town to share the Gospel. Every road into the town was marshalled by soldiers with guns. Helicopters were regularly overhead and the check points were heavily fortified with sandbags. The truth was that Crossmaglen was a sealed off town.

---

144 See Wikipedia for more information about Crossmaglen and the South Armagh Brigade of the IRA.
145 See RTE Archives – "Life in a Border Town 1977".
146 See Wikipedia – "Crossmaglen".

Ian watched the TV programme on Crossmaglen, referred to in the article above, with his mother in the family home. Ian said that the fire in the hearth was warming his feet, but the programme was warming his heart. He saw a need – "it was compelling." He started to pray for two things for Crossmaglen: that God would remind the people of Crossmaglen that He loved them and, secondly, God would send a very particular person to Crossmaglen – he had to be single and theologically trained. Ian said, "I remember the feeling when the penny dropped – that sounds like me!"

Motivated by the parable of the Good Samaritan, Ian went regularly to Crossmaglen in his mini-car with a passion to tell everybody that Jesus loved them, reassuring them of the Lord's compassion for them. There was fear in his heart as he began this mission: "Would I come back with my finger-nails intact? Would I actually come back?" Fear was associated with the name "Crossmaglen". With God's help and trust in God's word, Ian learned to overcome this powerful, penetrating fear that had kept other Christians away from this border town.

As he started to make weekly visits to the town, he knew that he was being closely monitored firstly, by locals who controlled the town, and secondly, by the British army. Actually, the army didn't know what to do with "this guy who was going around talking about God". He raised suspicions because he was not linked to any church or Christian organisation. He was an individual and a volunteer. The town generally did not have visitors and very few salesmen ventured into the area. The fear was that they would be thought to be there to gather information for the British army. Ian was "the stranger in town". Curtains were pulled back and people watched as he went from door to door, street to street sharing the love of Jesus.

Ian's identification was that of a Christian. He did not identify himself as a Protestant but as a disciple and follower of the Lord Jesus Christ. The neighbours that he had been brought up around thought he was mad: "Why are you going to a people who are trying to kill us?" To go to a mission field overseas was acceptable, but to go 29 miles down the road to a Republican, Catholic border town, whose culture was different to the one he was brought up in, was strange and difficult to understand.

The reality was that Protestant communities felt threatened by the republican paramilitary groups, but Catholic communities felt equally intimidated by the loyalist paramilitary groups. Both communities lived with fear and anxiety and dread of being attacked by an opposition group. Both communities were pawns in this civil war that was ravaging the island of Ireland. Both communities suffered needless and indiscriminate violence. There are grieving families in both communities.

There were two scriptures that guided and motivated Ian with this mission to Crossmaglen: Firstly, the parable of the Good Samaritan: the challenge was "to invest in the wounds of those on the other side and to do good". Secondly, I Corinthians 13:4-8: *"... love is kind... it keeps no record of wrongs ... love never fails."* Ian was convinced that God's love "could fill the vacuum of fear that was in Crossmaglen".

Ian has many God honouring stories of the mission he has led in Crossmaglen for over forty years now. Here are just a few:

During some follow-up visits to families, Ian was invited into one home where he was offered a bowl of soup. The grapevine advice for any visitor to Crossmaglen was: "don't accept any hospitality because they will put crushed glass in the soup and sandwiches that are offered to you". Faced with this dilemma the following scripture came into Ian's mind – Mark 16:18: *"... and when they drink deadly poison, it will not hurt them at all."* Ian took the soup and said, "That verse means that I can walk on landmines and they won't explode; I can take soup and trust God."

Visiting Crossmaglen another day, Ian noticed that nobody seemed to be at home. He went back to his car, which was parked in the town square, and asked the Lord, "What do you want me to do now?" The answer Ian received was, "Go home". Chuckling to himself, he drove away. When he arrived home, he saw a news flash: a bomb had gone off in the town square and that's where Ian's car had been parked. He now understood why he had no answers from the doors he had knocked. His father commented, "Well you came home, son."

Ian expanded his ministry into Crossmaglen by taking a stall at the local weekly market. He would sell clothes and second-hand Bibles. It was a way to meet more people and open doors to speak about the love of Jesus. One particular day he noticed that the market was quiet. Suddenly, there was a big bang and he saw that the army barracks had been hit by a rocket. Glass was flying everywhere and there was panic. Ian looked up and saw another rocket coming over the houses and lowering its path to hit the barracks again. Ian recalls that he "lifted up his hand toward the rocket and said, 'In Jesus's name be still". The rocket landed but did not explode." The shock and stress of the first rocket witnessed a lady collapse on Ian's stall. He said to her, "Don't worry, God is in control." Meanwhile, her son was saying, "Ma, ma, let's go and get out of here." The woman turned to her son and said, "This gentleman says God is in control." Ian said within himself, "I hope you are."

This mission of love into Crossmaglen continued to grow. A summer mission for children was started and continues to be held annually. A bus was turned into a mobile coffee bar and local teenagers would come. There would be discussions on the love of God. On one occasion, Ian left the bus to give a sausage to a passing soldier. The teenagers on the bus were booing and hissing. When Ian got back on the bus he said, "We are not here for sides, but here for lives. You may hate that soldier but God loves him."

There has been a personal cost during these forty years of ministry. Ian has been stoned as he has travelled to Crossmaglen; he has had cars stolen and later found burned out; fireworks have been put through his letter box; children's toys have been smashed and flowerbeds damaged and much more.

On one occasion Ian and the family came home from church and found their home had been burgled and the place was an utter mess, with very personal items left on display. Ian found this very hurtful. The sermon that Ian and the family had heard that evening in church was based on Romans 8:28: *"And we know that in all things God works for the good of those who love him…"* The local police said, on seeing the scene, "someone doesn't like you." One night, sometime later, a person turned up at the home and admitted to the crime. Ian's words to the person were, "I forgive you" and he gave this counsel to the person: "We don't need to go through what happened. You are forgiven and take this opportunity to go forward in your life." A guiding principle for Ian, in all the attacks and the intimidation has been, "choose life, not vengeance."

Ian has also had death threats and he admits that "they penetrated deep. They were very invading and destroying. It was like being bullied at school." Through the support of others and prayer, God really delivered him from these threats and their impact.

Ian sums it all up by saying, "We are here today by the grace of God; we are kept by the power of God for the purpose of the Kingdom of God. I am still excited."

Over past years he has received an MBE from the Queen, the Peace Prize from the USA and various others prizes such as the Nationwide Building Society, in recognition of the ministry in Crossmaglen.

Some recent news:

"Peacemaker Ian Bothwell opens new centre in Crossmaglen, South Armagh with Crossfire Trust.

"South Armagh peacemakers Ian and Pauline Bothwell opened a new centre in Crossmaglen yesterday, which they hope will mark a new phase of their work in the area. Journalist Paul Rooney cut the ribbon on the new premises purchased by South Armagh peacemaker Ian Bothwell of Crossfire Trust in Crossmaglen.

The couple have been working in South Armagh since the 1970s from their base in Darkley, under the banner of Crossfire Trust. Ian, who is originally from Tynan in South Armagh, went to bible college in the 1970s and later felt a vocational calling to South Armagh and Crossmaglen in particular.

Together, the couple and a large team of volunteers and supporters, offer a wide range of services to the community, including sheltered accommodation, help with furniture, clothing and food, as well as counselling.

Yesterday their vision of 20 years to open a base in Crossmaglen came to fruition when they cut the ribbon on their cafe and drop-in centre, 'Something More', on the site of the former post office."[147]

Through giving refuge to all; by providing counsel and help; by offering friendship and being an example of forgiveness; by showing acceptance and love; by being a witness to the power of the love of JESUS, Ian, his wife and the Crossfire team, faithfully year by year, through many trials have crossed over to the other side and invested in the hurt and pain of others and seen many lives changed and a whole community touched.

---

147 News Letter 5th June 2021: Philip Bradfield

Hope Now And For The Future

*"And the God of all grace, who called you to
His eternal glory in Christ, after you have suffered
a little while, will himself restore
you and make you strong, firm and steadfast."*
1 Peter 5:10

On January 8th, 1956, five missionaries were murdered trying to bring the Gospel of the LORD Jesus Christ to an indigenous tribe in Ecuador. The story made headlines for weeks. They all left behind them wives and four had young children. Here is an example of suffering, because of someone else's sin.

The five missionaries were Americans, between the ages of 27 and 32. Their names were Peter Fleming (27); Jim Elliot (28); Ed McCully (28); Roger Youderian (31) and Nathanael "Nate" Saint (32). Five women were left as widows and eight children were bereft of a father. One of the widows, Marilou McCully, was eight months pregnant at the time that "Ed" was murdered. The men were speared to death on a bank of the Curaray River, called "Palm Beach". After many weeks of dropping gifts from a plane in a bucket the men had decided to land the plane, believing the tribe to be friendly. They were murdered there on that riverbank.

What happened next is very challenging. In 1959, "Nate" Saint's sister, Rachel and Jim Elliot's widow, Elisabeth, made contact with the tribe and went to live amongst them. Rachel Saint remained there for thirty years.

Jim Elliot's daughter wrote, "After my father's death my mother got to know two Huaorani women who had fled the tribe because of violence. They said we want you, and the sister of Nathaniel Saint, we want you to come and tell our people about God. While we lived with them, and we were there almost two-and-a-half years, I of course got to know all of the tribe and the ten men who had done the killing. Amazingly, I really don't remember being afraid of them. They were always laughing and they would always make my mother laugh. So, I simply enjoyed being with them. Of course, it was a tragedy, and I often wish I had known my dad. Still odd. But I really believe that God allowed this to happen so that more and more people could actually see what real commitment to Christ means. And I really don't believe their lives were wasted."[148]

Steve Saint, one of Nate's Saint's sons and the nephew of Rachael Saint, was "adopted" by a man called Mincaye, the man who had killed his father. Steve spent summers with the tribe from the age of 9. Steve went on to work with them and set up a technology and education centre to develop their practical skills and gifts. James Boster, an anthropologist, who studied the history of the tribe concluded that Christian conversion prevented self-extinction. "Deadly cycles of revenge had scattered them into small, paranoid factions. Attempted truces failed because their language had no words for abstractions such as 'peace'. Because Christianity was brought by kin of men they had killed, but who befriended them in return, it became a powerful signal commitment to nonviolence."

Dr Boster, who is not an evangelical Christian, said further, "At first blush, their death was needless, as they were there on a mission

---

[148] Gledhill R. (2017), "I miss my father, but he gave his life for Christ", Christian Today.

of peace. But, in the long run, the fact that their kin went back in peace to teach was a strong signal that the tribe could trust both the messengers and the message."[149]

What about the Troubles in Northern Ireland? An often-used Bible scripture when individuals suffer heartaches and desperate circumstances is Romans 8:28: *"And we know that God causes all things to work for good to those who love God, to those who are called according to His purpose."* (NASB). We can see how that scripture has worked out in this example from South America. But what about Northern Ireland?

In the book "Considering Grace", the story is told of Alan McBride. Alan's wife, Sharon, and his father-in-law, Desmond, were murdered in the bomb attack at Frizzell's Fish Shop on the Shankill Road in 1993. Alan has gone through all the questions in searching for meaning behind this horrendous experience that brought him great pain and hurt. Shortly after his wife's murder he read this in a book, "God judged it better to produce 'good' from 'evil' than to suffer no evil to exist." Those words impacted him deeply. "This quote spoke to my soul in ways that other attempts at finding meaning had failed to do; be it the numerous conversations I had with friends and family, dozens of psychotherapeutic sessions or endless Sunday morning sermons at church."

Alan wrote further, "I never did find 'meaning' because sometimes there isn't any 'meaning' to be found. Nothing that could explain away the hurt and the pain and nothing that would ever make what happened on the Shankill Road that October day to be 'okay'."

---

[149] Rodgers A. (2006), "Ecuadoran tribe transformed after killing of 5 missionaries", Pittsburgh Post-Gazette

Where is Alan today? "…I think I can truthfully say I have moved on. Life is 'good' again. God is producing something good out of something that was horrible and hard. Sharon's death was still a senseless killing. They all were. All those killed in the 'Troubles' and all of those who have died since; the latest statistic being the journalist Lyra McKee."[150]

Today Alan is a committed peace campaigner. He has worked at the WAVE Trauma Centre in Belfast and with the YMCA. He was a founding member of Healing through Remembering and served on the Northern Ireland Human Rights Commission (2012-18).

These two stories illustrate how something good can come out of evil and result in God-honouring service. These stories give us hope. There have been many studies over the years that highlight how powerful hope can be in the most desperate of experiences. A noted physiologist wrote, "Hope, faith and a purpose in life, is medicinal. This is not merely a statement of belief but a conclusion proved by meticulously controlled scientific experiment."[151]

When I read the New Testament, the Christian truth of hope is broken down into different parts and together, they can be a powerful means of healing in the hearts of those broken by life and the evil of this world. Let me give you a sample of verses that speak of hope.

> John 16:33: *"I have told you these things, so that in me you may have peace. In this world you will have trouble. But take heart! I have overcome the world."*

---

150 Ganiel G. and Yohanis J. (2019) "Considering Grace: Presbyterians and the Troubles". Ireland, Merrion Press
151 Yancey P. (1990) "Where Is God When It Hurts", Michigan, Zondervan

> Colossians 1:27: *"To them God has chosen to make known among the Gentiles the glorious riches of this mystery, which is Christ in you, the hope of glory."*
>
> John 14:3: *"And if I go and prepare a place for you, I will come back and take you to be with me that you also may be where I am."*
>
> Hebrews 4:16: *"Let us then approach God's throne of grace with confidence, so that we may receive mercy and find grace to help us in our time of need."*
>
> Romans 5:5: *"And hope does not put us to shame, because God's love has been poured out into our hearts through the Holy Spirit, who has been given to us."*
>
> Matthew 5:4: *"Blessed are those who mourn, for they will be comforted."*

In our brokenness and despair, the mysteries of circumstances, the questions that arise, the suddenness and fragility of life, we have hope for the present and hope that stretches beyond the here and now and into eternity. I now want to lay out some of the truths about our hope – truths that will keep us holding on to the LORD; truths that will bring experiences into our lives during our dark days and nights; truths that will draw our minds to the LORD Jesus Christ.

The Holiness of God...

In recent years my wife, Pat, and I have experienced some dark and bleak times in our personal lives and in the family. These have been times of loss, heartache, personal examination, anger, hurt, pain, misinformation, betrayal and disconnection. Thank God, as I am writing this book, I can say that we have come from that dark place of a few years ago and we are now serving the LORD in a more fruitful and hope filled place. I remember a close friend of ours, speaking to us about the experiences of Job in relation to our own lives at the time. This friend believed that the LORD had directed her to Job as a means of encouragement for us. The LORD has restored and we are living in 2022 with hope and trust.

There was one truth that gripped my heart in early 2018 and the LORD has built on that truth in my life since: the truth that God is Holy. I wrote in my journal, "God is not nice: God is Holy." I grew in understanding the holiness of the LORD and started to see His holiness as a blessing. I noted actions and attitudes that I should express and live by in light of Him being Holy. In the midst of trying circumstances, I would say to myself, "God will never misuse me, abuse me or take advantage of me." God's holiness was a real comfort and strength during those years of bleakness and lostness. During 2018, Pat was travelling from Northern Ireland to England on a weekly basis to help care for our twin granddaughters. Before I took her to the airport on a Sunday to catch her plane we would pray and confess, "Lord you are Holy. Lord you are Sovereign." We would ask for a breakthrough in our lives week by week but then confess, "Lord you are sovereign. Lord you are holy."

The Breaking of Bread…

I know that different church traditions practice communion at various times in a year. The tradition I was part of for many years celebrated the breaking of bread on a weekly basis.

Further, there are a wide range of views about the place of breaking of bread in a local church. Some suggest that it only has a memorial dimension. When we break the bread and drink the wine, we are just remembering an historical event. It was a tremendous historical event, but was it only an event? Again, the tradition that I come from would have taught that the communion is a means of grace. The preaching of God's Word, the fellowship of believers, worship, intercessory prayer and the laying on of hands are other examples of activities which are a means of grace.

Means of grace are disciplines that brings the LORD into our lives; disciplines where the spiritual becomes real; disciplines where the LORD Himself imparts something of Himself by the Holy Spirit into our hearts.

When we come to the breaking of bread with our pains, our hurts and heartaches, what should we be thinking and expecting?

Firstly, what comes to mind, is the terrible suffering that Jesus went through on the Cross. We tend to gloss over the physical agony that must have racked his body for hours. It was all done by wicked men. I don't think we will ever get to the bottom of understanding the depth of emotional pain and hurt that Jesus felt, abandoned by his disciples but more, abandoned by His Father. "Where are you?" Jesus said. In the depths of agony and not fully understanding, as a human being, the agonies that he had to go through for His Father, he cries, "Why have you forsaken me?" When we break bread, let us remember and take encouragement that the questions and the feelings that arise in us because of horrific experiences, have been felt by Jesus too.

Secondly, we can expect the LORD to minister to us. On one occasion whilst breaking bread as a local church, some members of the congregation smelt a perfume and an aroma filling the place. It was the LORD. In the worship of remembering his horrific death, the LORD revealed Himself present. Isn't that what we long for in the midst of our pains and hurts? LORD reveal your presence.

Thirdly, it would be good to remember this truth: Jesus still bears the scars but the wounds are healed. I honestly can't remember if I have read that truth somewhere or whether it is original. Original or not, it is true. This truth about Jesus is an encouragement and a reality check. Pat and I will never forget the hurts and the nights of pain we went through in past years but, we don't dwell on what happened. We have moved on. The wounds have healed.

The Present Ministry of Jesus…

Essential though it is, I get weary when I hear leaders continually taking a congregation back to the Cross. Jesus is involved in much more now. His life and His purpose didn't stop at the Cross but the Cross was a door into a "much more" ministry which is a blessing to us today. Hebrews 8:6 expresses this:

> *"Now, however, Jesus has received a much more excellent ministry, just as the covenant He mediates is better and is founded on better promises."* (BSB)

I keep a journal. On the February 13th, 2018 I wrote, "Feeling a little desperate about our situation." I was trying to prepare some ministry because I was preaching at a local church in the evening. I wrote this later in the day, I am now "feeling upbeat and hopeful." I noted the time; it was 4.45pm. I wrote, "Who has been praying for me?" and then this thought came into my mind, "Marcus, Jesus has been praying for you." My heart leapt for joy and that truth never left me. On the January 30th, 2019, I wrote in my journal, "Thank God, Jesus is praying for us as a family. Praise God: shout it from the roof tops!"

Hebrews 4:15-16 also speaks of Jesus' resurrection ministry for us:

"For we do not have a high priest who is unable to sympathize with our weaknesses, but we have one who was tempted in every way that we are, yet was without sin. Let us then approach the throne of grace with confidence, so that we may receive mercy and find grace to help us in our time of need." (BSB)

In those circumstances, where we have more questions than the answers; in the desperate, heartbreaking happenings we have hope because Jesus is praying for us.

The Eternal Viewpoint...

Paul writes in 2 Corinthians 4:17-18,

"For our light and momentary affliction is producing for us an eternal weight of glory that is far beyond comparison. So we fix our eyes not on what is seen, but on what is unseen. For what is seen is temporary, but what is unseen is eternal..." (BSB)

A Christian friend of mine lost his granddaughter a number of months ago. She was 36 years of age. She also was a Christian. He told me how he went in prayer to the LORD about his granddaughter's death. This was the comforting word that was spoken into his spirit: "You look at things from the earthly, I look at things from the eternal."

Nicky Gumbel writes, "A one-year-old boy shattered his back falling down a flight of stairs. He spent his childhood and youth in and out of hospital. Gavin Reid, the former Bishop of Maidstone, interviewed him in church. The boy remarked, 'God is fair.' Gavin asked, 'How old are you?' 'Seventeen,' the boy replied. 'How many years have you spent in hospital?' The boy answered, 'Thirteen years.' Gavin asked, 'Do you think that is fair?' He replied, 'God has got all of eternity to make it up to me.'

We live in a world of instant gratification that has almost entirely lost its eternal perspective. The New Testament is full of wonderful promises about the future: all creation will be restored. Jesus will return to establish 'a new heaven and a new earth' Revelation 21:1. There will be no more crying, for there will be no more pain and suffering. Our frail, decaying mortal bodies will be changed into a body like that of Jesus' glorious, resurrected body.

Suffering is not part of God's original created order (see Genesis 1–2). There was no suffering in the world before rebellion against God. There will be no suffering when God creates a new heaven and a new earth (Revelation 21:3–4). Suffering is, therefore, an alien intrusion into God's world.

> Psalm 16:8-11 says, *"I keep my eyes always on the Lord. With him at my right hand, I will not be shaken. Therefore, my heart is glad and my tongue rejoices; my body also will rest secure, because you will not abandon me to the realm of the dead, nor will you let your faithful One see decay. You make known to me the path of life; you will fill me with joy in your presence, with eternal pleasures at your right hand."*

This is one of the few Old Testament passages that foresees the hope of eternity in the presence of God. David writes, *"Because you will not abandon me to the grave, nor will you let your Holy One see decay. You have made known to me the path of life; you will fill me with joy in your presence, with eternal pleasures at your right hand"* (vv.10–11).

This is our future hope. These verses show that the resurrection of Jesus was foretold in the Scriptures (see Acts 2:25–28). This life is not the end. You can look forward to an eternity in the presence of God, to fullness of joy and pleasures forevermore. *"Our present sufferings are not worth comparing with the glory that will be revealed in us"* (Romans 8:18).[152]

I can remember going through a deep period of depression in my life. I would break down in tears for no reason. The doctor wanted me to take three months off from my work as a pastor. I felt that I couldn't but agreed to cut back drastically on my workload. The doctor explained the imbalances that were in my body and he prescribed a tablet for me to take. Each day, before I took the tablet, I would thank God for the medicine. Further, I would practice a certain discipline in my devotions. As David stood before the Lord, I would do the same. I would come and say to the LORD, "Here I am again, sitting before you."

I came out of that period of depression and I remember something my wife said to me after a prayer meeting: "Marcus you are not so harsh in your praying. You are gentler and softer." In the months of depression, when I didn't know if I was on my head or my feet at times, God had worked in my heart and changed me.

There is another truth to highlight here. It is an aspect that we can quickly forget. The LORD is preparing us for eternity. The LORD has an eternal plan for our characters and lives. It is a plan that involves us being an exhibition of His grace. It is a plan that we will be "to the praise of His glory."

The Practice of Lament…

Jack Hayford has written a book called, "How to Live Through a Bad Day."[153] The subtitle of the book is "7 Encouraging Insights

---

152 Gumbel N. Day 26 "Why Does God Allow Suffering" Bible in One Year
153 Hayford J. (2001) "How to Live Through a Bad Day", Nashville, Thomas Nelson, Inc.

from Christ's Words on the Cross." Jesus cried from the Cross, "My God, My God, why have You forsaken me?" Matthew 27:46 (NKJV) Hayford writes, "Aim your hard questions at God, not man."

The Psalmist David first made this cry to the LORD. (Ps 22:1). Hayford writes, "That was the cry of the psalmist in the spirit of the privileged candor that God welcomes from those who worship Him. He welcomes tears in His presence, for He isn't their source, and he allows complaints, for He alone can meet the needs. Another example of David crying out or lamenting before the LORD is in Psalm 142:1-2: *"I cry aloud to the LORD; I lift up my voice to the LORD for mercy. I pour out my complaint before him; before him I tell my trouble."*

Hayford writes, "Again, the message is clear: Aim your hard questions at God. You may not get the answer right then, but you can count on two things: (1) your cry never will fall on deaf ears, and (2) time will always bring an answer in your best interests. Always."

It has been noted that two-thirds of the psalms are laments. These psalms give us instruction about crying out to God in our anguish and despair. "They give us permission to rage and wonder and question where God's at and ask why he seems silent and absent when life doesn't make sense."[154]

What makes lament, a lament? How does a lament differ from just having a "pity party"? How can a lament be different to just venting our gripes? In the Old Testament we read about Israel complaining vigorously against the LORD. They were thinking the worst about the LORD. They were testing the LORD. They were putting the LORD "in the dock". They were doubting His character. They were

---

[154] Ochstein S. (2020) "Hope for the Future: How the psalms of lament encourage us that our pain isn't the end of the story" medium.com/interfaith

throwing their accusations at the LORD. In their eyes, God was guilty. That is not how to lament.

What is a lament? "A lament is an appeal to God based on confidence in His character."[155] A lament is mourning in the presence of God. Matt and Beth Redman's song expresses praise and worship in the mist of sorrow and pain. These are the words of it, [156]

Blessed Be Your Name

Blessed Be Your name in the land that is plentiful,
Where Your streams of abundance flow,
Blessed be Your name.
And blessed Be Your name when I'm found in the desert place,
Though I walk through the wilderness,
Blessed Be Your name.

Every blessing You pour out, I'll turn back to praise.
When the darkness closes in, Lord, still I will say,
Blessed be the name of the Lord,
Blessed be Your name.
Blessed be the name of the Lord,
Blessed be Your glorious name.

Blessed be Your name when the sun's shining down on me,
When the world's 'all as it should be',
Blessed be Your name
And blessed be Your name on the road marked with suffering,
Though there's pain in the offering,
Blessed be Your name.

---

155 Packham G. www.ntwrightonline.org/five-things-to-know-about-lament
156 Redman M. and B. (2005) "Blessed Be Your Name", London, Hodder & Stoughton

Every blessing You pour out I'll turn back to praise,
When the darkness closes in, Lord, still I'll say,
Blessed be the name of the Lord,
Blessed be Your name.
Blessed be the name of the Lord,
Blessed be Your glorious name.

You give and take away,
You give and take away,
My heart will choose to say
"Lord, blessed be Your name."

Psalm 77 is a Psalm of lament. The writer is desperate, groaning, and in distress but then turns his mind to the LORD: *"To this I will appeal; the years of the right hand of the Most High."* The writer remembers the works and the miracles of the LORD; *"Your ways, O God, are holy. What God is so great as our God?"* The Psalm starts with cries and feelings of faintness, but takes refuge in the unfailing love and mercifulness of the LORD.

Sara-Louise Martin, in her story, speaks of how the psalms of lament brought her solace and understanding in the midst of her grief.

Christian author, Glenn Packham writes this: "Lament in the Bible is not simply an outlet for our frustrations. Though venting may be proven to be beneficial in and of itself, a lament is a form of prayer. And prayer is not passive. Many of the laments in the psalms are calls to action. They plead with God to pay attention to them and to act on their behalf. In fact, many Old Testament scholars identify "petition" as an essential element of a lament Psalm."[157]

---

157 Packham G. www.ntwrightonline.org/five-things-to-know-about-lament

Jesus cried out to the LORD, *"My God, My God, why have You forsaken Me?"* Matthew 27:46 (NKJV). We will never experience the depths of anguish and pain that Jesus expressed with this gut-wrenching cry on the Cross, but we have all had, and will continue to have experiences where we just cry out, "Why, God?" Our encouragement is that we have a Saviour who has said the same thing to the LORD and understands this cry of our hearts.

Regarding this piercing cry, Hayford encouraged us to "Aim (our) hard questions at God." But how did it all end for Jesus? We remember the great shout, *"It is finished"* John 19:30 (NKJV). He didn't say, "I am finished", meaning the anguish and pain has finished me off. But his final words were, *"Into Your hands I commit my spirit"* Luke 23:46 (NKJV)). This was a statement of trust. "He was surrendering His control of life into the Father's hands…His words of trust, surrendering everything into the strong hands of the almighty God, ARE His concluding lesson to us about how to live through a bad day."[158]

Psalm 23 is a favourite psalm of many people and verse 4 is very well known: *"Even though I walk through the valley of the shadow of death, I will fear no evil, for you are with me; your rod and your staff, they comfort me."* The Psalmist went through the *"valley of the shadow of death"* but the LORD was with him.

Philip Greenslade comments, "We need laments because we need a way of dealing with strong negative emotions. The choices are few. Either we suppress the pain, which is psychologically harmful, or we vent it on others, which is socially destructive. There is another way. We can express it honestly and fiercely to God. This is precisely what the lament prayers of the Psalms allow – indeed encourage – us to do. Evidently the psalmists believed that God had a great shock-

---

[158] Hayford J. (2001) "How to Live Through a Bad Day", Nashville, Thomas Nelson, Inc.

absorbing heart. They sensed His love well enough to believe that He could cope with their most outlandish questions, unreasonable doubts, and even angriest cries for vengeance."[159]

How can our laments be honourable to the LORD? How can we ensure that our laments do not become a moaning session? There are two things on which we can found our songs of sorrow. Firstly, the sovereignty of God and, secondly, His unfailing love for us. In our dark nights, we tell HIM that He is LORD. In the deep sadness of our soul, we confess that HIS love for us is the love of a Father for his children.

Forgiveness...

> "Forgive us our debts, as we also have forgiven our debtors."
> Matthew 6:12

I have read many stories of the people who were directly affected by the Troubles: people who lost sons and husbands and brothers and sisters; people who have lived with tremendous pain because of injuries they suffered. Approximately 52% of the people killed during the Troubles were civilians. "The paramilitaries and the security forces may have been the adversaries, but the death toll was highest among the civilian population amidst which that low-intensity war was fought."[160] They were people who were often in the wrong place, at the wrong time – people who were going about their lives but became involved in bomb attacks.

Although it may take time and is never easy, people can, by God's grace, come to a place of forgiveness, even after suffering great trauma

---

159 Greenslade P. (2003) "Songs for all Seasons", Surrey, CWR
160 Henderson D. and Little I. (2018), "Reporting the Troubles 1". Newtownards, The Blackstaff Press.

in their lives. Rodney Wilson, Paul Elliott, David Clements, Maggie Burrows and Sara-Louise Martin, whose stories you have read, are outstanding examples of this.

Derek Prime writes, "God's forgiveness places an obligation upon us to forgive others. Living as some of our brothers and sisters in Christ do in brutal and war-torn environments where awful atrocities take place, this is no easy duty. We do not naturally possess the ability to forgive. Our natural human reaction to any wrong done to us is summed up in an inscription found on the monument to Sulla, a prominent statesman, in Rome: 'No friend ever did me so much good, or enemy so much harm, but I repaid him with interest.' But as Christians we do not forgive because it is easy, but because it is commanded."[161]

The People of God...

Rodney Wilson wrote, "We were always conscious of being carried by prayer from the many churches and prayer groups throughout the land and further afield in those dark days." Rodney was thankful for the invaluable help the family received on the farm from local Christians. Paul Elliott told the story of how one local church went way beyond "and bent over backwards" to help the family purchase another property in Armagh. The family moved to this new home within a year of the father's murder. It meant a fresh start.

Sara-Louise Martin, in her story, highlights how God's love in action really can change lives.

"There have been people who have encouraged me over the years. When someone has a history of loving and supporting you, you're

---

161 Prime D. (1996) "The Lord's Prayer for today" Bromley, Day One Publications

more likely to allow them to speak into your life when things are tough – they have gone the distance.

There were people who slipped me bible verses. In my teens and twenties when I was trying to figure out what to do with my life, there were people who prayed me through various transitions."

God's people can be a means of grace. They are a key to healing and restoration for those who have suffered deep trauma and are living with a broken heart.

The Holy Spirit...

Rob Warner writes, "When I was a young Christian, the Holy Spirit had me confused. In one Bible study on Acts chapter 2, the group leader said, 'Let's not talk about the Holy Spirit. It's too controversial!' I didn't know much about the Spirit, but I knew that if He was important in the New Testament, He be should be important to me."[162]

It is sad that the person and work of the Holy Spirit has been a topic for debate for the Church over many centuries. Has Jesus wept over the church, just as He wept over Jerusalem, because of the arguments that have gone for years and years about the place and the ministry of the Holy Spirit in this age of grace?

In this book about suffering and, in this chapter about hope, why is the person and work of the Holy Spirit so important for us?

When Jesus was talking to the disciples about the Holy Spirit, he said, *"And I will ask the Father, and he will give you another Counsellor to be with you forever – the Spirit of truth."* John 14:16-17.

---

162 Warner R. (1997) "Alive In The Spirit" London, Hodder and Stoughton Ltd.

The word "another" carries the meaning of "just like". Jesus is saying that the Holy Spirit is going to be "just like me." That is very relevant for us as we face suffering and heartbreak in this life. The agenda that the LORD God gave Jesus is described for us in Luke 4:18-19: *"The Spirit of the Lord (is) upon Me, because He has anointed Me to preach the good news (the Gospel) to the poor; He has sent Me to announce release to the captives and recovery of sight to the blind, to send forth as delivered those who are oppressed (who are downtrodden, bruised, crushed, and broken down by calamity)."* (AMP) Let us remember that behind every healing, deliverance and miracle Jesus manifested on earth, there was a family who had been broken by an illness or sickness that had gripped someone dear to them. We see a compassionate Jesus reaching out to the individual, and, as a consequence, reaching out to the family.

Jesus tells us, the Holy Spirit, is going to be "just like me." He is going to be caring, compassionate and present with us in our troubles.

Ruth, whose husband was a policeman, was murdered leaving her widowed with three young children. She not only had to deal with her own grief but the heartache of her children. Ruth said this about her experience of prayer: "When you were praying, it was like you were talking to your best friend. Maybe you didn't get an answer straight away, but you knew that somebody was listening."[163]

Janet, whose husband suffered severe injuries from a bomb planted under his car, said this about her experience of prayer following this attack: "I couldn't sleep so I just prayed most of the night, off and on. It was actually a really good time because you were so close to God then that you felt you could have reached out and touched him."[164]

---

[163] Ganiel G. and Yohanis J. (2019) "Considering Grace: Presbyterians and the Troubles". Ireland, Merrion Press

[164] Ganiel G. and Yohanis J. (2019) "Considering Grace: Presbyterians and the Troubles". Ireland, Merrion Press

What does the word "Counsellor" mean when used about the Holy Spirit? This word can be translated as Comforter and Divine Helper. The word literally means, "one called alongside to help." In our sufferings and heartaches the Holy Spirit comes alongside to help. The stories of Ruth and Janet testify to the work of the Holy Spirit in coming alongside to help and comfort.

There is a verse in Romans which helps us further to understand where and how the Holy Spirit can help us. Paul writes, *"...the Spirit helps us in our weakness. We do not know what we ought to pray for, but the Spirit himself intercedes for us with groans that words cannot express."* Romans 8:26

There is one further, relevant work of the Holy Spirit in our lives for us to consider. The Bible was written by people under the guidance and inspiration of the Holy Spirit. That is an accepted belief in Evangelical and Pentecostal circles. I believe we need the author of the Bible to be at work in our hearts and minds also. The Holy Spirit knows the Bible inside out and from back to front. He knows what scriptures to lift from the pages of the Bible to comfort and guide us in our sufferings.

At the end of 2019, I had preached a message in the church we were attending in Devon, entitled, "When God messes with our plans." It was a Christmas message based on the LORD turning the plans of Mary and Joseph upside down. After preaching the message, I remember thinking – is the LORD speaking to us regarding our plans for the future? Is the LORD going to shake them? And that is exactly what happened in the following 18 months. Different challenges came along and by the beginning of 2021 we were facing decisions about our future. But the Holy Spirit prepared the way by giving me, at the end of 2019, a number of confessions to make over lives. I would have declared these statements daily and some days, in 2020 and early 2021, were dark. The confessions were:

Psalm 140:6	*"You are My God."*
Revelation 4:4	*"Holy, Holy, Holy is the LORD."*
Nehemiah 4:14	*"... the LORD (will) fight for (us)..."*
Psalm 52:8	*"I trust in God's unfailing love for ever..."*

The Holy Spirit was making the words of the Bible alive and relevant in the circumstances we were in as a family. We didn't know the whys and wherefores, but these confessions helped us stay before the LORD. I am reminded of something that a friend said, "Not everything that goes wrong is a mistake!"

By the beginning of March 2021, we had an idea of the decisions that faced us and the order in which they had to be made. The Holy Spirit spoke to me on the 4th March from Exodus 13:17-18 and the way the LORD had led Israel the long way round after their deliverance from Egypt. The Holy Spirit helped me to understand something of the journey we had been on since the end of 2017.

God is God...

There is, understandably, great disappointment that many individuals who committed some of the terrible atrocities in Northern Ireland have never been brought to justice. The sadness is that many of these individuals are still walking the streets of the province, while the victim families only have a grave to visit. Many churches across Northern Ireland have plaques commemorating the violent deaths of some whose lives were taken.

Although justice is important, the main stories that I have told in this book confirm how individuals have taken refuge in God and are leaving ultimate justice in his hands. Ian Bothwell said, "People don't need a day in court but they need a day in church."

Ross, a Christian, who lost his brother in the Troubles, said, "There mightn't be justice here and now, but in the long term, justice will be done. A sovereign God has all things in the palm of His hands. That makes it liveable – to a point."[165]

The LORD God is a God of Justice. There is a day coming when the LORD God is going to *"judge the living and the dead."* Acts 10:42, 2 Tim 4:1, 1 Pet 4:5. When we all appear before HIM, he will not "fly off the handle". God's judgement will not be vindictive; it will not be capricious; it will not be selective. The writer of Ecclesiastes states, *"For God will bring every deed into judgement, including every hidden thing, whether it is good or evil."* 12:14 (NIV) We will all appear to answer for our actions in this life. His judgement will be in line with His Holiness. There will be no "ifs" and "buts". There will be no extenuating circumstances. God will know all the motivations and attitudes of our hearts. Upon His judgement, there will be no appeal.

In regard to the Troubles, governments will be judged for their failures to act justly. During those terrible years, there was a "dark side" to what happened. None of this has passed the LORD God. Individuals who plotted and planned and carried out devilish deeds will stand before the LORD for their actions.

"The LORD will not leave the guilty unpunished." Nahum 1:3

But the story doesn't end there. Christians have a hope in the LORD Jesus Christ, who rose from the dead and ascended back to Heaven.

Mrs Brown, whose husband, Harold, was murdered in Mountain Lodge Pentecostal Church, said to a journalist who had come to the family home, "… we are not grieving, son. We are rejoicing that

---

165 Ganiel G. and Yohanis J. (2019) "Considering Grace: Presbyterians and the Troubles". Ireland, Merrion Press

Harold is with the Redeemer right now. You see Harold was ready to be with the Lord as all the people were in that hall.' Then she smiled and said, 'You see, I know where he is right now.'" [166]

Nora Bradford, whose husband, Robert, was murdered, wrote, "My love for the Lord means I know Robert's safe and can't be harmed any further and, in fact, is happier than he's ever been, living, smiling and laughing in the beautiful place called Heaven, totally present with his King."[167]

For those Christians who were murdered or suffered terrible injuries and subsequently died, they had this hope, "We are confident, yes, well pleased rather to be absent from the body and to be present with the Lord. 2 Corinthians 5:8 (NKJV)

Packham concludes, "Because Jesus Christ is risen from the dead, we know that sorrow is not how the story ends. The song may be in a minor motif now, but one day it will resolve in a major chord. When every tear is wiped away, when death is swallowed up in victory, when heaven and earth are made new and joined as one, when the saints rise in glorious bodies... then we will sing at last a great, 'Hallelujah!'"[168]

A Story: "It is Well with my Soul"

The hymn, "It is well with my soul" is a favourite of many Christians. It is a hymn that came out of some tragic circumstances. The story behind the hymn is "one of the most heartrending stories in the annals of hymnody.

---

[166] Henderson D. and Little I. (2018), "Reporting the Troubles". Newtownards, The Blackstaff Press
[167] Bradford N. (2021), "When Time Is Taken", Belfast, Maurice Wylie Media
[168] Packham G. www.ntwrightonline.org/five-things-to-know-about-lament

The author, Horatio G. Spafford (1828-1888), was a Presbyterian layman from Chicago. He had established a very successful legal practice as a young businessman and was also a devout Christian. Among his close friends were several evangelists including the famous Dwight L. Moody, also from Chicago.

Spafford's fortune evaporated in the wake of the great Chicago Fire of 1871. Having invested heavily in real estate along Lake Michigan's shoreline, he lost everything overnight. In a saga reminiscent of Job, his son died a short time before his financial disaster. But the worst was yet to come.

Hymnologist Kenneth Osbeck tells the story: "Desiring a rest for his wife and four daughters, as well as wishing to join and assist Moody and (his musician Ira) Sankey in one of their campaigns in Great Britain, Spafford planned a European trip for his family in 1873. In November of that year, due to unexpected last-minute business developments, he had to remain in Chicago, but sent his wife and four daughters on ahead as scheduled on the S.S. Ville du Havre. He expected to follow in a few days.

On November 22nd the ship was struck by the Lochearn, an English vessel, and sank in twelve minutes. Several days later the survivors were finally landed at Cardiff, Wales, and Mrs Spafford cabled her husband, 'Saved alone.'"

Spafford left immediately to join his wife. This hymn is said to have been penned as he approached the area of the ocean thought to be where the ship carrying his daughters had sunk.

Another daughter, Bertha, was born in 1878 as well as a son, Horatio, in 1880, though he later died of scarlet fever. After the birth of daughter Grace in 1881, Spafford and his wife moved to Jerusalem out of a deep interest in the Holy Land. There they established the American

Colony, a Christian utopian society engaged in philanthropic activities among Jews, Muslims and Christians.

After decades of benevolent activities, the Colony ceased to be a communal society in the 1950s, though it continued in a second life as the American Colony Hotel, the first home of the talks between Palestine and Israel that eventually led to the 1983 Oslo Peace Accords."[169]

Horatio Stafford died of malaria on 16th October 1888, four days before his 60th birthday. He was buried in the Mount Zion Cemetery in Jerusalem.

This is a very sad story but a hymn was written out of this tragedy that has been a comfort to many people over many years. I remember when my mother was diagnosed with lumps on her vocal chords and the doctor's advice was not to talk for three months. It was a very trying time in the family home but I can remember being in our local church and in the stillness of a worship service, one Sunday morning, my mother started to sing, "It is well, it is well with my soul." It was awe inspiring and many in the service were blessed.

The Stafford family suffered a heartrending experience but their legacy has been a tremendous blessing – not only the hymn but the mission that was set up in Jerusalem. Their tragedy didn't end with bitterness, but was turned into something to bless others.

It Is Well With My Soul

When peace like a river attendeth my way,
When sorrows like sea billows roll

---

[169] See umcdiscipleship.org

Whatever my lot, Thou hast taught me to say
It is well, it is well with my soul

It is well (it is well)
With my soul (with my soul)
It is well, it is well with my soul

Tho' Satan should buffet, if trials should come
Let this blest assurance control
That Christ hath regarded my helpless estate
And has shed His own blood for my soul

My sin, oh the bliss of this glorious thought
My sin, not in part, but the whole
Is nailed to the cross, and I bear it no more
Praise the Lord, praise the Lord, O my soul

For me, be it Christ, be it Christ hence to live!
If Jordan above me shall roll.
No pang shall be mine, for in death as in life
Thou wilt whisper Thy peace to my soul.

But Lord, 'tis for Thee, for Thy coming we wait,
The sky, not the grave, is our goal:
Oh, trump of the angel! oh, voice of the Lord,
Blessed hope! blessed rest of my soul.

H.G. Stafford / P.P. Bliss

A Challenge

Thank you for buying this book and persevering to this final chapter. I trust that I have been successful in weaving the theme of suffering into the chapters and stories I have included. The Christian life is not some wonderful breeze but it comes with heartaches, pains and sufferings. Life is filled with unfairness. Suffering is a big player in the Christian life but, with the LORD, there is a path through the pains and we don't have to stay in a place of bitterness.

It has been a great privilege to be involved with this project and to speak to the individuals whose stories are at the centre of the book. Thank you for letting Pat and me sit down with you and talk about the most heartbreaking experiences of suffering in your lives. It was a privilege to listen to your stories. It was also a very humbling experience.

The interviews and the material I have researched for this project present a different picture of Christianity in Northern Ireland to the harsh, unforgiving and judgemental one that has too often been evident. I heard from people about their trust in the Lord Jesus. I heard about them not looking for justice now, but leaving it to the sovereignty of God. I heard about different church groups reaching out to the victims and quietly going about supporting them and being there for them. I heard about God's healing work in their hearts and how, despite the pain, they have been able to move on with their lives. The memories are still there; there is still sadness but, in Paul's words, they have *"reached out for what is ahead."* Using their own experiences, they have been able to come alongside others in their pain and grief.

I trust that the stories in this book will also challenge you to move forward with God's purpose for your life. Bad things do happen to good people, but those things are not to define us and put our life on standstill. God calls us to trust in Him. Ask for His grace to help and say, "LORD, what do you have for me to do for You?" God has some amazing people in His kingdom. We will probably never hear of many of them this side of Heaven. He has such people in Northern Ireland. Pat and I met with some and our prayer is this: "LORD in a province that is still suffering and aching from the past, please raise up more people to witness to your healing power. You do have a life of purpose beyond the events of the past."

Contact The Author

authorMarcusThomas@gmail.com

Inspired To Write A Book?

Contact
Maurice Wylie Media
Your Inspirational Christian Publisher

Based in Northern Ireland and distributing around the world.
www.MauriceWylieMedia.com

www.ingramcontent.com/pod-product-compliance
Lightning Source LLC
Chambersburg PA
CBHW041141110526
44590CB00027B/4087